The Hiker's Guide
to NEVADA

by
Bruce Grubbs

FALCON™

Falcon Press® Publishing Co., Inc.
Helena, Montana

Falcon Press is continually expanding its list of recreational guidebooks using the same general format as this book. All books include detailed descriptions, accurate maps, and all information necessary for enjoyable trips. You can order extra copies of this book and get information and prices for other Falcon books by writing Falcon Press, P.O. Box 1718, Helena, MT 59624. Also, please ask for a free copy of our current catalog listing all Falcon Press books.

ISBN 1-56044-205-0
Library of Congress Catalog   Card Number 92-059954

Printed in the United States of America.

Falcon Press Publishing Co., Inc.
P.O. Box 1718, Helena, MT 59624

All text and maps, by the author.
Photos by author except as noted.
Cover Photo: by Bruce Grubbs, Wheeler Peak Trail, Snake Range, Great Basin National Park.

 Text pages printed on recycled paper.

CONTENTS

SOUTHERN

ACKNOWLEDGMENTS

I wish to thank my friends and hiking companions over the years who suggested new areas to hike and often accompanied me in the backcountry.

Specifically, I wish to thank the personnel of the U.S. Bureau of Land Management, the U.S. Fish and Wildlife Service, the USDA Forest Service, the National Park Service, and the Nevada Division of State Parks for their valuable contributions, as well as Ron Kezar for his contribution. Thank you to Marjorie Sill, who wrote the afterword, "Nevada's Wilderness Challenge." The book would not have been possible without their help.

Sincere thanks to Duart Martin for invaluable proofreading and editing, and to Stewart Aitchison for suggesting the project and providing assistance along the way.

And finally, I wish to thank my editor, Randall Green, and all the fine folks at Falcon Press who made this guide a reality.
—*Bruce Grubbs*

Mule deer browsing in the predawn chill near the Baker Lake Trail, Great Basin National Park. The diamond-shaped sign near the aspen trunk marks a snow survey course used by the federal Soil Conservation Service to measure winter snow pack. This information is used to predict spring runoff, vital information for the desert settlements dependent on mountain water.

PREFACE

Nevada, the Silver State, is associated more with mining and gambling than with hiking in many people's minds. But most of Nevada is rugged backcountry where the rich contrast between valley and mountain is most apparent to an explorer on foot. Nevada has desert salt flats shimmering in the sun and cool mountain streams cascading down rocky slopes, shady redrock canyons and dramatic alpine peaks, quaking aspen, and the ancient bristlecone pines.

A Nevada hike can vary from an easy stroll on an interpretive nature trail to a strenuous multi-day backpack trip. Hikes of both extremes as well as intermediate walks are represented here. This book is an invitation to escape from the man-made world and discover a world where nature still dominates and time runs on a far slower scale.

The Monitor Range from Monitor Valley. The 10,000-foot plateau of Table Mountain runs twenty miles north to south, forming the main crest of the Monitor Range. Numerous trails lead to this scenic alpine plateau.

HIKE LOCATIONS

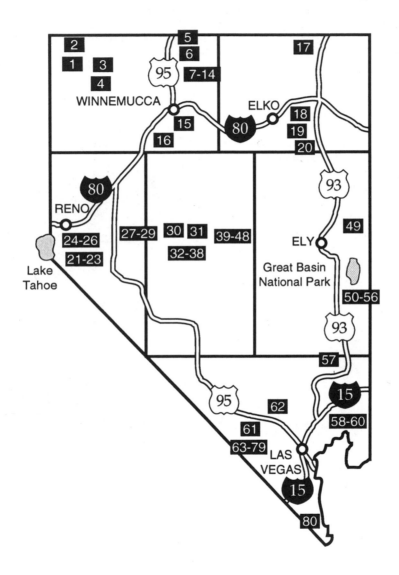

INTRODUCTION

Hiking in Nevada

This book is a sampling of the hiking and backpacking available in Nevada. An attempt has been made to include the widest possible variety of hiking, not only to benefit you, the reader, but also to publicize areas of the state in which hiking is threatened by non-compatible uses. Little-known and less traveled hikes are represented as well as more popular areas. Relevant natural and human history of the area is included with many of the hike descriptions. Use this book as a starting point for your own explorations of this varied region of the Southwest.

Geology and Geography

Most of Nevada lies within the portion of the American West known as the Great Basin, an area that includes parts of California, Oregon, Idaho, Wyoming, and Utah. Within the Great Basin, all mountain drainages flow into closed valleys, or basins, and no water reaches the sea. More than 160 parallel mountain ranges, all trending north-south, drain into some ninety valleys. The majority of these isolated mountains are in Nevada. While a few valleys do contain lakes, most feature salt flats instead, where stream flows from the mountains have evaporated, leaving behind a crust of white minerals.

Nevada's elevation ranges from just 300 feet above sea level to more than 13,000 feet. The average elevation is approximately 5,500 feet. The lowest valleys and mountains are in the southern and western part of the state, with elevations increasing toward the north and east. The Snake Range is the most lofty in the state, culminating in the glacier-carved summit of Wheeler Peak.

Millions of years ago during the formation of the North American continent, the area that is now Nevada was stretched from east to west by crustal forces. Numerous north-tending fractures, or faults, formed as the rocks broke under the strain. Some of the resulting blocks sank to form the valleys, while others rose to form the mountains. As the faulting continues to lower the basins and raise the mountains, erosion from water flowing downhill tends to wear down the mountains and fill the valleys. The topography we see today reflects the fact that the faulting is still active enough to keep the mountains from being worn down to a flat plain.

More recently, as these events go, a colder and wetter climate caused snow to accumulate in the higher ranges and form glaciers. The last of these ice ages ended about 10,000 years ago but left its mark on the topography in the form of steep, glacially carved mountain peaks and classic U-shaped mountain valleys. As the climate warmed and the glaciers receded, the massive flow of meltwater collected in huge lakes rivaling the Great Lakes in size. In many parts of Nevada, the ancient shorelines of these lakes are clearly visible as terraces along the lower mountain slopes.

During the cooler glacial climate, extensive forests covered the valleys and bordered the lakes. As the last ice age gradually ended, the warming climate caused plants and animals, which had adapted to a cooler, wetter climate to migrate up the mountainsides.

Nevada hikers have a surprising abundance of backcountry possibilities from which to choose. Here a hiker climbs above timberline on Toiyabe Summit Trail.

Natural History

Most wet weather reaches Nevada from the west and northwest in the form of Pacific storms. Much of the moisture from these winter storms falls on the high Sierra Nevada and the Cascade Mountains before reaching Nevada. The moisture that is left tends to fall on the mountains rather than the valleys. Precipitation, mostly in the form of snow, varies from five inches in the driest valleys to eighteen inches in the higher eastern Nevada ranges. Temperatures range from forty below zero up to 115 degrees Fahrenheit. Much of Nevada is too hot for enjoyable hiking in the summer, and some of it is too cold in the winter. The best hiking seasons are spring and fall, but because of the great elevation range the higher mountains are best in summer, and the lower deserts are best enjoyed in winter.

This great variation of climate within the state makes life interesting for the native plants and animals as well. Most plants and many animals are adapted to a limited range of temperature and moisture, and so different communities are found at various elevations in the valleys and mountains. Valleys in central and western Nevada feature tough desert shrubs—shadscale, bud sage, greasewood, and salt bush. Lower valleys in southern Nevada are covered with creosote bush, mesquite, and the striking Joshua tree, while the higher valleys are dominated by sagebrush. This shrub-grassland covers nine-tenths of the state.

The most common animal is jack rabbit, but coyotes, gophers, red foxes, and western badgers also may be found. Antelope and wild horses favor the open valleys, while mule deer range from desert to mountain depending on the season. Generally, the reptiles prefer the deserts—these include rattlesnakes as well as harmless snakes and numerous varieties of lizards.

Wheeler Peak, at 13,063 feet is Nevada's highest mountain but not its highest point. That honor goes to Boundary Peak, a northern outlier of the White Mountains that lies mostly in California. A good trail leads to the summit but caution must be used whenever snow covers the higher slopes. Stewart Aitchison photo.

Although the North Twin River Trail meanders through tall shady aspens for several miles, the much drier sagebrush and mountain-mahogany slopes are never more than a few yards away.

Most of the mountain ranges are covered with forests, and the type of trees vary with elevation and location. Many of the valley animals can be found here as well—raccoons, porcupines, skunks, squirrels, and chipmunks. Along the western border, the trees of the Sierra Nevada dominate, with ponderosa, Jeffrey, and sugar pines constituting the forest from about 5,500 feet to 7,500 feet elevation. Above 7,500 feet, red fir, western white pine, and lodgepole pine become common up to about 9,000 feet. A subalpine forest of whitebark pine, lodgepole pine, and mountain hemlock continues to timberline at about 10,500 feet. Above this elevation is arctic-like tundra.

The central and southwestern ranges have the unique Great Basin forest zones with dwarf pinyon pines and juniper trees between about 7,500 feet and 8,500 feet elevation. Above and extending to about 10,000 feet are mainly shrubs such as mountain mahogany and sagebrush. The subalpine forest reaches 11,500 feet and consists of limber pine and bristlecone pine. The gnarled, tough bristlecones are the oldest living things on Earth.

Eastern Nevada ranges have a Rocky Mountain forest sequence, with the lowest zone being pinyon-juniper, topped by ponderosa pine, then Douglas-fir and white fir. The subalpine forest consists of subalpine fir, Englemann spruce, limber pine, and bristlecone pine. Also, elk and bighorn sheep generally prefer the rugged mountain slopes.

Throughout the state, mountain streams are bordered by aspen, alder, chokecherry, cottonwood, water birch, and willow. These locations are favored by beaver as well as many bird species. Rainbow trout have been introduced to many streams throughout the state. Surprisingly, waterfowl are common along the desert lakes and marshes, and the rarity of desert water makes this habitat all the more precious.

Human History

It appears that the first humans arrived in Nevada between 13,000 and 10,000 years ago, probably as a result of migrations from Siberia via the Bering Strait. Numerous archaeological sites are helping to tell the story of early man in Nevada (These sites are protected by Federal law, and if they are disturbed, another piece of the story is gone forever). The timing of man's arrival coincided with the end of the last ice age and the last of the great glacial lakes. These early people took advantage of the easy living provided by the lakes, catching fish as well as hunting native species of the American horse and camel. Other human inhabitants appeared to specialize in hunting mammoths. Most lived in caves or crude shelters, but toward the end of the prehistoric period, around A.D. 1000, a Pueblo culture of well-organized communities developed. Some of these sites contained well over a hundred houses.

After about A.D. 1100, the more advanced communities were abandoned, for unknown reasons. Some of the people may have migrated elsewhere, and some probably became the ancestors of the tribes discovered by Europeans.

Four major Native American groups occupied Nevada, with the Southern Paiutes probably being the first tribe encountered by Europeans at the southern end of the state. The Northern Paiutes occupied the western third of Nevada, and the Western Shoshones roamed the eastern half. A smaller group, the Washoes, ranged along the eastern Sierra Nevada.

By the time the white man arrived, the Nevada climate made it difficult for the natives to wrest a living from the land. Most of the Native Americans were hunter-gatherers, migrating constantly to take advantage of the seasons.

Quaking aspens grow quickly in areas cleared by fire or avalanche, and live only about 100 years. The bark is easy to carve and a tempting signboard for travelers. Sheep herders, miners, and ranchers all recorded their travels on the graceful white trunks. A practice that was harmless when few people were in the country but becomes vandalism when large numbers of people do it. Carving on aspens or defacing any natural feature is rightly illegal in Great Basin National Park. This carving dates from 1909 according to the inscription.

Recreation time was probably limited to harvest gatherings or communal hunts.

Probably the first European to enter Nevada was Father Francisco Garces, part of a larger Spanish expedition seeking a more direct route from Santa Fe to Monterrey in 1776. Competition between British and American fur trappers heated up in 1826, when Jedediah Smith led an expedition across the southern tip of Nevada to California, then crossed the central part of the state from west to east. Another trapper, Peter S. Ogden, entered northern Nevada in 1828 and worked his way south and east to Utah. Further explorations by Ogden opened up the route along the Humboldt River across the northern third of Nevada, a route later used by wagon trains of emigrants headed for the Pacific Coast.

The earliest emigrants were trespassing on Mexican soil, but by 1850 Nevada was part of the American Territory of Utah. Discovery of gold in California caused the tiny trickle of emigrants to become a flood. Most of the parties used the Humboldt River route, still a major corridor of travel across Nevada.

Inevitably, trading posts sprang up along the emigrant trails, while others stayed behind to try their hand at ranching and mining. By 1860 when Nevada became a territory, significant deposits of gold and silver had been discovered in the Virginia City area—the Comstock Lode. This caused rapid population growth, and Nevada became a state in 1864. In comparison, neighboring Arizona Territory did not become a state until 1912.

Although ranching has been a staple of Nevada life since the early settlers arrived, mining has been responsible for most of the economic activity until recently. Although the boom-and-bust economy of mining has made life difficult for many Nevada communities, many Nevadans still view mining as essential to the state's welfare.

Since 1945, gambling, retirement communities, and tourism have tended to supplant mining as the major source of income. Increasingly, Americans see the undeveloped portions of Nevada as precious areas to be protected and enjoyed in their natural state. The recent establishment of Great Basin National Park, Nevada's first National Park, has won support from local communities and is rapidly becoming a popular destination for tourists as well as hikers.

Ruins such as this one in the Toiyabe Range are protected by the federal Antiquities Act, which is intended to preserve our archaeological heritage.

HIKING TECHNIQUES AND ETHICS

Family Hiking

Hiking with children should be fun. This does not mean that it cannot be challenging for the youngster, but it should be something that can be accomplished and still be enjoyable. Where the hike takes place and what is expected to be seen will add much to the experience for a child.

There are many good camping and hiking areas in the state where children can experience the fun of seeing a beautiful flower, butterfly, babbling brook, or watch a blue bird bring food to its young. To see a deer bounding away in a woodland setting can be very exciting for child or parent.

Each season presents an entirely new experience on the same trail. The seasonal cycle brings spring flowers with migrating and nesting birds, summer with young wildlife and more flowers, fall colors and southward migrating birds, and completing the cycle with winter snow.

Many trails provide access to good fishing and hunting areas, ideal places for outings. They are ideal for one-day trips. It is important to make the hike fun, especially for smaller children. Until the children get older and are able to keep up with their parents, forget about that long hike to a backcountry campsite. Instead, plan a destination that is only a mile or two from the trailhead. Kids tire quickly and become easily sidetracked.

Help children enjoy the hike by pointing out special things along the trail. You will soon learn that they will be pointing out interesting things to you. If you have hiked the trail before, help them by anticipating what is around the next bend—a pond wriggling with tadpoles or a mountain stream with interesting insects under the rocks. If you make the hike fun, kids will stay interested and keep going.

Careful planning that stresses safety will help make your trip an enjoyable one. Biting insects—mosquitoes, gnats, and flies, can destroy a trip. Be prepared with an effective repellent that you have tried on the kids ahead of time. It is too late when you are on the trail to find out that the repellent is more irritating that the bugs. DEET is the effective ingredient in most repellents. However, prolonged overuse of thirty percent DEET can cause some reactions in children. To ease parents' concern with the stronger repellent, two products have been introduced, one called Skedaddle and the other Skintastic, have 6.5 percent and 7.5 percent DEET respectively. Although not quite as effective as stronger DEET concentrations, they are useful and less irritating to children.

Be especially watchful for stinging insects—wasps, hornets, bees, and ants. The first-aid kit should contain an effective topical ointment to relieve the pain of stings.

It is also important to have comfortable clothes suitable for the season. Be aware that children can be more sensitive to cold than adults and prepare for it. Properly fitting shoes will help prevent blisters on young, tender feet.

Set up a tent at home and consider spending a night or two in it so your child can grow accustomed to your backcountry shelter. A flashlight can help

Using modern lightweight equipment, it is possible to camp in comfort with almost no impact on the country. Good sleeping pads mean a good night's rest with no need to scar the fragile alpine tundra, and lightweight stoves eliminate the need to build campfires.

with temporary fear of the dark. Kids seem to prefer rectangular sleeping bags that allow freedom of movement. Don't forget a knit cap for the child to wear in the sleeping bag on cool nights. It will help greatly to keep the young one warm.

Children learn from their parents by example. Hiking and camping trips are excellent opportunities to teach youngsters to tread lightly and minimize their imprint on the environment.

There may be extra hassles involved with family hiking trips, but the dividends are immeasurable. Parents will gain a rejuvenated perspective of nature, seen through the eyes of a child, that will reward them each time they venture out on the trail.

Leave nothing but footprints...

Although the Native Americans and the early explorers and settlers lived off the land out of necessity, the modern hiker and backpacker finds maximum freedom in being virtually independent of the land. Carrying food, shelter, and warmth in a reasonably light pack, the walker needs only water and a level place to sleep. This lightweight camping style means a camp can be established or broken in a matter of minutes rather than hours, leaving little trace of the hiker's presence. The ability to "leave nothing but footprints" could hardly have come at a better time. The shrinking American wilderness is under increasing pressure as a steadily growing population discovers the joy and serenity to be found in the outdoors. In the last century, a small population of miners easily destroyed much of Nevada's mountain forests. Today, those same mountains can provide recreation for a much larger population if each person will treat the countryside with respect.

While walking, stay on established human or animal trails if available, and avoid cutting switchbacks. Members of a large party traveling cross-country should spread out rather than create a new trail by walking single file. These practices minimize soil erosion. In the Great Basin, the soil is often protected by a crusty surface composed of lichen and moss, which effectively slows erosion but takes years to reform once disturbed.

Very few hikers will deliberately litter, and much of what we see along the trail is accidental or the result of ignorance. Orange peels, for example, take a long time to decompose in the dry climate. Individual hikers can put an end to the litter problem by packing out a bit of someone else's litter at the end of each hike.

Look for campsites that are "hard," such as sand, gravel, or hard dirt. With the better sleeping pads, even solid rock slabs make comfortable campsites and offer the additional freedom to move around camp barefoot. Soft campsites, such as meadow grass or pine needles, must be used with great care to avoid destroying the ground cover. Rather than constructing a level bed or tent site look for a natural one. Avoid having to dig drainage ditches by choosing a slightly elevated site where rain water will run away from your shelter. In heavily used areas use an existing campsite rather than starting a new one. One of the major reasons people avoid old campsites is the litter and campfire rings left by old-style "heavy" campers. If time and load permits clean up a messy campsite and leave a pleasant surprise for the next party. Ashes can be buried, blackened rocks scattered, and trash packed out if loads are light.

Although many hikers enjoy the freedom and relaxation of cooking meals

11

on a backpacker's stove, for others a campfire is an essential part of the experience. In some situations, campfires should not be built, such as in heavily used areas or near timberline where wood is scarce and where prohibited by regulation. During the summer, the fire danger may be extreme, and no fire should be built on a windy day. Most of the time, it is possible to be a responsible hiker and still have a campfire.

Use an established campfire ring if available. Otherwise look for a site in gravel, sand, or bare soil. Then dig a shallow pit, heaping the dirt around the edges to form a wind and fire break. Do not use stones, which become permanently blackened. Collect dead wood from the ground or the lower parts of trees by breaking by hand. If you need an ax or a saw, either the wood is too large or too scarce. Keep your fire small, both to avoid using large amounts of wood and to keep the amount of ashes small. Most backpacker's trash is so light it can be easily carried out. But paper can be burned to reduce bulk. Note that many paper packages are lined with aluminum foil, which does not burn.

When ready to leave camp make certain the fire is cold by mixing in water or dirt and stirring until there is no obvious smoke or heat. Then check with your bare hand, cover the fire pit with the dirt from the original pit, and scatter any remaining wood. After a short time, your fire site will again look natural.

If lightweight food is carried (modern supermarkets are full of convenient items that make ideal backpacking food) and carefully repacked to eliminate excess packaging, the trash resulting from even a week or more in the backcountry can easily be carried out. Avoid burying food, because animals will find it by smell shortly after you leave and dig it up. But contrary to popular opinion, the food will probably not get eaten. Human food is not usually appetizing and certainly not good for wildlife.

Wilderness sanitation is the most critical skill needed to keep the backcountry pristine. A walk in any popular recreation area will show that few people seem to know how to relieve themselves away from facilities. In some areas, naturally occurring diseases such as Giardiasis are being aggravated by poor human sanitation. Fortunately, the rules are simple. If facilities are available, use them. Their presence means that the human population of the area is too large for the natural disposal systems of the soil. In the backcountry select a site at least a hundred yards from streams, lakes, and springs, then dig a small "cat-hole" about six inches deep into the organic layer of the soil. Some people carry a small plastic trowel for this purpose. Avoid barren, sandy soil if possible. When finished, fill the hole, covering any toilet paper. Burning toilet paper is a good idea only in moist areas where there is no fire danger.

Our archaeological and historical heritage

In the backcountry, the hiker will encounter artifacts of various ages. Some of these structures, tools, and other artifacts date from before European discovery of the Americas. Others were built by early settlers and explorers. All are valuable links with our history and prehistory. Yet increasingly this evidence of early civilization is being destroyed by vandals. Federal laws have been passed to protect such antiquities, but ultimately the responsibility must lie with the users of the backcountry. Keep in mind that the relationships between artifacts in a site are often more important than the artifacts themselves. Petroglyphs and pictographs (rock drawings) have lasted thousands of years but are easily destroyed by thoughtless people.

MAKING IT A SAFE TRIP

Wilderness is a safe place to be. Nature is indifferent to hikers in the sense that there are neither malevolent or beneficial forces. The hiker must be self reliant but there is no need to be paranoid. Once a hiker develops confidence in his or her techniques, abilities, and equipment, then operating in the back-country becomes a welcome relief from the complex tangle of civilized living. Wilderness decisions are usually important but also basic. While "out there," things that seemed important in civilization lose some of their urgency. In other words, we gain a sense of perspective.

Many wilderness accidents are caused by individuals or parties pushing too hard. Set reasonable goals, allowing for delays from weather, deteriorated trails, unexpectedly rough country, and dry springs. Be flexible enough to eliminate part of a hike if it appears that your original plans are too ambitious.

A few plants are hazardous to the touch, such as poison ivy and stinging nettle. Spiny plants like cactus are easy to avoid. Never eat any plant unless you know what you are doing. Many common plants, especially mushrooms, are deadly.

Animals will leave you alone unless molested or provoked. Do not ever feed wild animals, as they rapidly get used to the handouts and then will vigorously defend their new food source. Around camp, problems with rodents can be avoided by hanging food from rocks or trees. Even the toughest pack can be wrecked by a determined mouse or squirrel who has all night in which to work. Heavily used campsites present the worst problems, but in Nevada there's not much reason to camp in heavily used areas. Rattlesnakes cause concern but can easily be avoided. They usually warn off intruders by rattling well before you reach striking range. Since rattlesnakes can strike no further than half their body length, avoid placing your hands and feet in areas you cannot see and walk several feet away from rock overhangs and shady ledges. Snakes prefer surfaces at about eighty degrees Fahrenheit, so during hot weather they prefer the shade of bushes or rock overhangs, and in cool weather will be found sunning themselves on open ground.

Water

In the desert, water is the most important consideration in planning a hike. On day hikes make certain you carry enough water. In hot weather, as much as two gallons per person per day may be required. On desert backpack trips, the route and itinerary are planned around water sources. It is convenient but not always possible to be near a spring or stream for lunch stops and at camps. Collapsible water bags that will hold up to two gallons are available and should be carried in addition to reliable plastic water bottles. Collapsible containers make it possible to carry water for a dry lunch or even a dry camp. Dry campsites are often very pleasant places such as ridges and hill tops. However, plan to reach at least one reliable water source per day, unless the weather is cool and you are experienced in dry camping.

Springs and streams shown on maps are often unreliable. The newest USGS topographic maps no longer clearly show the difference between permanent and seasonal stream beds. The best way to determine the reliability of desert water sources is through experience in the area, either yours or that of a trusted

Hikers should be prepared for snow on the higher peaks at any time of the year. Cliff Leight photo.

friend. Allowance must be made for springs and streams that may be dry: Do not depend on any single water source. Be aware of reliable water sources that are off your route. Known water sources are listed in each hike description; there may be more water sources, but I have attempted to err on the side of caution.

Very few backcountry water sources are safe to drink. The exceptions are isolated springs and direct snow melt. Contamination has resulted from wild and domestic animals as well as the increasing human population. Infections from contaminated water are uncomfortable and can be disabling. Giardiasis, a severe gastrointestinal infection, has been receiving more attention. However, recent evidence indicates that humans have probably been blamed for more than our share of responsibility, as the cysts that cause Giardiasis are spread by all mammals. Nevertheless, there is no doubt that poor backcountry sanitation has contributed to the problem.

So unfortunately, the rule must be: Purify all water sources unless very sure they are uncontaminated (Water containing Giardia cysts or other disease agents may be sparkling clear and cold). Iodine water purification tablets, available from outdoor shops, are very effective. (See *Medicine for Mountaineering* in "Further Reading") One iodine tablet will kill most problem organisms, including Giardia cysts, in one quart of water. Read and carefully follow the directions on the bottle. Note that the tablets must be kept dry to retain their effectiveness.

Filters have become increasingly popular, especially with large parties. Most filters are heavier than iodine tablets, but produce equally safe water at lower cost and with less iodine aftertaste.

Chlorine tablets are not reliable for purifying wilderness water due to the common presence of organic matter (bits of leaves, etc.) that are harmless but use up the purifying agent. Also, chlorine tablets rapidly lose effectiveness once the original bottle is opened.

Weather

Nevada has an intermountain climate. The dry clear air allows strong radiation cooling during the night so that temperatures often drop fifty degrees Fahrenheit by sunrise. Even the hottest areas generally have cool nights. Also, temperatures drop about five degrees Fahrenheit for each thousand-foot rise in elevation, so mountain tops are often much cooler than lower slopes.

As mentioned earlier, Nevada receives most of its precipitation as snow, generally during the winter months. However, snow may fall at any time of year on the higher mountains. Be prepared by bringing more warm clothing than what appears you will need. During the cooler season, consider synthetic garments made of polypropylene or polyester fibers. These fibers retain their insulating ability when wet better than any natural fiber, including wool. Avoid continuous exposure to chilling weather, which may subtly lower body temperature and cause sudden collapse from hypothermia, a life-threatening condition. Cool winds, especially with rain, are the most dangerous because the heat loss is insidious. Hypothermia may be completely prevented by wearing enough clothing for warmth and wind protection to avoid chilling and by eating and drinking regularly to keep the body fueled.

Spring, summer, and fall are generally dry, though summer thunderstorms may develop, especially in southern and eastern Nevada. Since much hiking is in the mountains, lightning can present a hazard. Less obvious are the

Sunrise at North Twin River trailhead, Toiyabe Range. Nevada's dry, stable weather means that camping can often be done without a tent.

hazards associated with sudden heavy rain, which include flash flooding and rapid temperature drops. Keep in mind that the mountains are eroded mostly during spring runoff and flash floods. Avoid camping in stream beds and dry washes.

In hot weather, water is vital. Ensure that you have a reliable supply and then drink enough to satisfy your thirst and then some. Remember if it gets too heavy in your pack you can always drink it. Your body will use it efficiently.

Protection from the heat and the sun is important. Most people find a lightweight sun hat vital for desert hiking. During hot weather, plan hikes in the higher, cooler mountains instead of the low desert, or hike early in the day to avoid the afternoon heat. Summer backpack trips can be planned to take advantage of the long days by hiking from first light to mid- morning, taking a long, shady lunch break, and then finishing the day's walk in early evening when it cools off. At dusk, keep an eye out for rattlesnakes, as they are active in the evening during hot weather.

Finding and Using Maps

Each hike in this book is accompanied by a map showing the access roads and the specific trail or route mentioned in the hike description. These maps are intended as general guides. More detailed maps are listed in the heading and referred to in the description of each hike and will be useful or even essential.

Topographic maps published by the U.S. Geological Survey are usually the best for hiking. These maps are published in sheets, or quadrangles covering relatively small areas. Topography is shown in detail by means of contour

Many Nevada trails are faint from lack of use, which makes them all the more attractive to hikers from heavily used areas. Rock cairns such as this one in the Monitor Range are commonly used to mark the trails.

lines, as well as manmade features such as trails, roads, buildings, etc. This information is very accurate at the date of publication shown on the lower right corner of each map. Unfortunately, the sheer number of maps (several thousand to cover a western state) makes updating a slow process. So trail and road information is often outdated. Many outdoor shops and some engineering and blueprint shops carry USGS maps. They are also available directly from the Geological Survey (see Finding Maps).

Other useful maps are published by the USDA Forest Service and the U.S. Bureau of Land Management. These maps cover a larger area and are updated more often, though the topography is usually not shown. They are best used in conjunction with topographic maps. These maps are usually available from the office listed under the heading in each hike description, from some outdoor shops, and from the regional or state offices of the land management agencies (see Finding Maps).

Trail signs are rare along many Nevada trails, and the hiker should carry topographic maps and a compass, and learn map reading skills well.

MAP LEGEND

◯ Described Trailhead

△ Camp Site

▪ Building

☐ Ruin

▲ School

) (Pass or Saddle

◣ Mountain

⚲ Springs

⬬ Lake

(200) State or Other Principal Road

[200] Forest Road

(200) U. S. Highway

(200) Interstate

▬▬▬ Paved Road

= = = = = = = = = : Dirt Road

- - - - - - - - - - Trail

.... Cross-Country Route

～～～ River, Creek Drainage

NEVADA

Trail Location Symbol

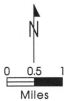

N

0   0.5   1
Miles

Map Scale

NORTHWEST NEVADA

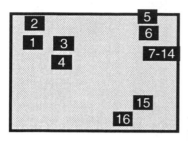

1. Desert Trail—High Rock Canyon Section
2. Desert Trail—Sheldon National Wildlife Refuge Section
3. Blue Lakes
4. Duffer Peak
5. Buckskin Mountain
6. Lye Creek Basin
7. Granite Peak
8. Rebel Creek Trail
9. McConnell Creek Trail
10. Horse Canyon Trail
11. Falls Canyon Trail
12. Santa Rosa Summit Trail—Buffalo Canyon
13. Santa Rosa Summit Trail—Singas Creek
14. Santa Rosa Summit Trail—North Hanson Creek
15. Water Canyon
16. Star Peak

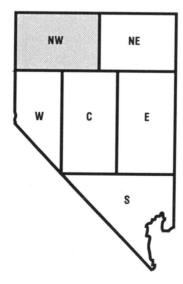

THE HIKES

The hikes are rated for relative difficulty as easy, moderate, or difficult. An easy hike is one with little elevation change, covering short distances, and normally on a maintained trail. Nearly anyone should be able to do these hikes. Moderate hikes should also be within most people's abilities, but will be longer and have more elevation change. The hiker should be prepared to spend part or all of the day on a moderate hike. Hikes rated difficult involve major elevation change, long distances, and possibly cross-country hiking. These hikes should be attempted only by experienced hikers.

Please be aware that the perceived difficulty of a hike varies with the individual hiker, the load being carried, the season, and the amount of trail maintenance.

HIKE 1 *DESERT TRAIL—HIGH ROCK CANYON SECTION*

General description: A multi-day backpack trip along the remote Desert Trail.
General location: 53 miles southwest of Denio, Nevada.
Maps: High Rock Lake 7.5-minute, Mahogany Mtn. 7.5-minute, Yellow Hills East 7.5-minute, Yellow Hills West 7.5-minute, Badger Mtn. SE 7.5-minute USGS; Desert Trail Guide, High Rock Canyon Section, Desert Trail Association.
Difficulty: Difficult.
Length: 32 miles one way.
Elevation: 4,910 to 6,160 feet.
Special attractions: A major section of the proposed National Scenic Desert Trail through the historic High Rock Canyon area.
Water: Stevens Camp.
Best season: Spring and fall.
For more information: Desert Trail Association, P.O. Box 537, Burns, OR 97720; no phone; Bureau of Land Management, Winnemucca District Office, 705 E. 4th St., Winnemucca, NV 89445; (702) 623-1500.
Permit: None.

Finding the trailhead: From Denio Junction, the southern trailhead may be reached by following Nevada Highway 140 southwest nine miles, then turning south onto graveled Road 34A. Continue about thirty miles through the Summit Lake Reservation. Continue another fourteen miles south-southwest to High Rock Lake.

From Cedarville, California, the southern trailhead can be reached by following California Highway 299 east-northeast for ten miles to the Nevada border, then continue on the graveled road for about eleven miles to Road 34. Follow the gravel road southeast about forty-three miles to Road 34A. Turn northeast onto 34A and continue approximately thirteen miles to High Rock Lake.

From Gerlach, the southern trailhead can be reached by following Road 34 north approximately thirty-four miles. This road is maintained. Turn off

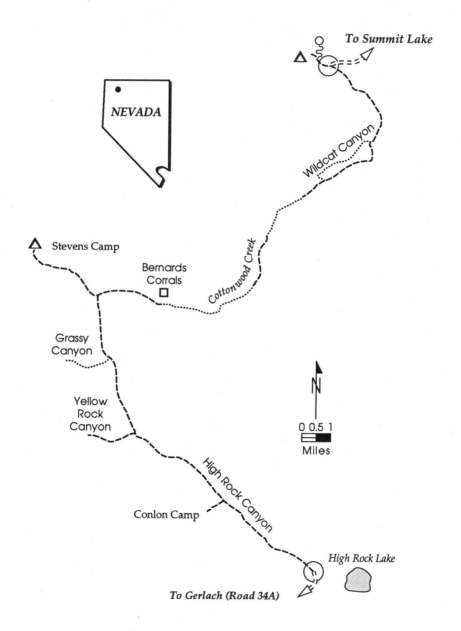

To Summit Lake

NEVADA

Wildcat Canyon

△ Stevens Camp

Bernards
Corrals

Cottonwood Creek

Grassy
Canyon

N

0 0.5 1
Miles

Yellow
Rock
Canyon

High Rock Canyon

Conlon Camp

High Rock Lake

To Gerlach (Road 34A)

Road 34 to the northeast onto Road 34A and continue approximately thirteen miles to High Rock Lake.

From Denio Junction, the northern trailhead may be reached by following Nevada Highway 140 west about thirty-four miles. Turn southwest onto the dirt road (not maintained) for about five miles, then turn south on Road 8A. Continue on the dirt road about eight miles to the Summit Lake sign and turnoff. Follow it southeast approximately twelve miles then turn southwest at the fork in the road. Continue about two miles to the spring at Cottonwood Canyon on the southern boundary of the Sheldon National Wildlife Refuge.

From Cedarville, California, the northern trailhead may be reached by following California Highway 299 east-northeast ten miles to the Nevada border. Continue east on maintained Road 8A for approximately forty-three miles, then turn onto the dirt Summit Lake road. Continue twelve miles then turn southwest at the fork in the road and continue two miles to the spring at Cottonwood Canyon on the southern boundary of the Sheldon National Wildlife Refuge.

The hike: The Desert Trail is not a constructed trail or clearly defined path. Usually it is a corridor without specific borders through which the hiker may pass, choosing his or her own route. The purpose is to avoid leaving a beaten path by minimizing the impact of the hiker on fragile soils and vegetation. The Trail in High Rock Canyon follows a road, while the northern part of the Trail follows both roads and Cottonwood Creek. It is highly recommended that you have the topographic maps for navigation purposes.

High Rock Canyon was the route of the Applegate Trail, a major emigrant trail connecting California and Oregon with the eastern states. The route was discovered by an Oregon party led by Jesse and Lindsay Applegate in 1846. Their intent was to discover an alternative to the already established Oregon Trail to avoid the dangerous Columbia River and to avoid threats from the British. Many people expected war to break out between the United States and Great Britain over the bitterly disputed Oregon Territory, and the American settlers were looking for a route that would not be subject to control by the British Hudson Bay forts along the Oregon Trail. The Applegate Trail was used sporadically at first due to Indian troubles, but by 1849 was well established. It continued to be the main route into and out of southern Oregon throughout the 1860s, until modern roads and railroads appeared.

The sheer rock walls of High Rock Canyon, as high as 800 feet in places, are composed of numerous volcanic lava flows, starting about 10 million to 25 million years ago. More recent volcanic activity and the effects of erosion have carved the lava into awesome gorges. The upper layer of dark basaltic rocks is from the final lava flow. The underlying distinct red band is a layer of fine soil that was baked by the intense heat as the molten lava moved across the earth. Beige bands beneath the red zone are volcanic ash deposits.

High Rock Canyon has been protected from grazing since 1984 in order to protect one of the last major examples of a native desert rye grass ecosystem. The Great Basin giant rye, tall sagebrush, and rice grass are prevalent. Willows are coming back along the riparian (streamside) zone and erosion is decreasing.

About 100 deer live in the canyons year-round, and 450 antelope spend the winters on the neighboring tablelands and benches. Golden eagles, prairie falcons, diverse species of hawks, and great horned owls make their nests on the steep canyon walls. Because birds of prey are so sensitive to the presence of humans, during the spring and summer nesting period, care must be taken to minimize disturbance of these majestic inhabitants. A raptor may leave its nest when humans are in the area, not returning until the visitor has left. A long absence from the nest could result in death for the eggs or newborn.

The U.S. Bureau of Land Management also manages the tablelands adjacent to the canyon to maintain about a hundred wild horses.

This hike description follows the Desert Trail south to north. From High Rock Lake hike northwest on the road about a mile to a gate with a "Welcome to High Rock" sign by the Friends of High Rock. Proceed northwest up the canyon along the dirt road. After a short distance, you enter the spectacular High Rock Canyon. About 4.5 miles from the entrance gate, Mahogany Canyon opens to the west and makes an interesting side hike. A jeep road goes 0.3 mile up Mahogany Canyon to Conlon Camp. The cabin here could be used as shelter in an emergency.

The main trail continues up High Rock Canyon. After about one mile, Pole Canyon opens to the north. It is not currently open to hiking due to private land.

Yellow Rock Canyon enters from the west, 9.5 miles from the gate, offering another possible side hike. About three miles up High Rock Canyon, Grassy Canyon enters from the west providing yet another side hike.

Continue up High Rock Canyon another three miles. Here the main trail follows a dirt road east out of High Rock Canyon. If desired, you can hike about four miles up High Rock Canyon to Stevens Camp, which has water. This side hike adds about eight miles to the total hike.

Continuing on the main trail hike east 2.5 miles on the dirt road to its end at Bernards Corrals. On the remaining section of the hike be aware that the trail passes near several sections of private land. Although public access is established for the Desert Trail, private land is not open for hiking off the trail.

From Bernards Corrals, the route is mostly along Cottonwood Creek. If it is dry, it may be easier to hike in the sandy creek bed. About 2.5 miles from the corrals, the creek turns generally northeast. Continue about three miles to the point where the Cottonwood Creek trail turns north and joins a jeep road, skirting the east side of the Yellow Hills. There are numerous other creekbeds that join Cottonwood Creek, so it may be advisable to use a compass and the topographic map along this section of the trail.

Hike north on the road for a little over two miles, staying east of a knoll. Here you leave the road to rejoin Cottonwood Creek. Follow the creek northeast about two miles until you come to three forks of Cottonwood Creek. Now hike east about 0.25 mile to a dirt road. This is to avoid the private land in Shoestring Valley. It is a good idea to consult the topographic map in this section. There should be a fork in the road near where it is first reached. Take the right fork northeast about 1.5 miles to another road that runs east to west. Cross this road then stay on approximately the 5,700 foot contour and hike northwest about 0.5 mile to Wildcat Canyon. This spectacular gorge contains a large shady cave. The cave is also an example of vandalism to an archaeological site.

The road parallels the gorge making it possible to avoid Wildcat Gorge if desired. The hiking distance is about the same. Follow Wildcat Gorge northeast about 2.5 miles until you reach a road in section 22. Follow the road for about four miles as it turns northwest and rejoins Cottonwood Canyon at the southern boundary of the Sheldon National Wildlife Refuge. This is the northern trailhead. There is a spring on the refuge about a mile northwest of the trailhead where camping is allowed. This would be an excellent spot to end your hike.— *Desert Trail Association*

HIKE 2 *DESERT TRAIL—SHELDON NATIONAL WILDLIFE REFUGE SECTION*

General description: A multi-day hike along the remote Desert Trail.
General location: 10 miles west of Denio, Nevada.
Maps: Badger Mtn. SE 7.5-minute, Rock Spring Table 15-minute, Big Spring Butte 15-minute, Railroad Point 15-minute, Denio 15-minute, Van Horn Basin 7.5-minute USGS; Desert Trail Guide, Sheldon National Wildlife Refuge Section, Desert Trail Association.
Difficulty: Difficult.
Length: 65 miles one way.
Elevation: 4,300 to 6,780 feet.
Special attractions: A major section of the proposed National Scenic Desert Trail through the Sheldon National Wildlife Refuge.
Water: No reliable sources. It is advisable to cache water in advance by vehicle.
Best season: Spring and fall.
For more information: Desert Trail Association, P.O. Box 537, Burns, OR 97720; no phone; Sheldon National Wildlife Refuge, P.O. Box 111, Lakeview, OR 97630; (503) 947-3315.
Permit: None.

Finding the trailhead: From Denio Junction, the southern trailhead may be reached by following Nevada Highway 140 west about thirty-four miles. Turn southwest onto the dirt road (not maintained) for about five miles, then turn south on Road 8A. Continue on the dirt road about eight miles to the Summit Lake sign and turnoff. Follow it southeast approximately twelve miles then turn southwest at the fork in the road. Continue about two miles to the spring at Cottonwood Canyon on the southern boundary of the Sheldon National Wildlife Refuge.

From Cedarville, California, the southern trailhead may be reached by following California Highway 299 east-northeast ten miles to the Nevada border. Continue east on maintained Road 8A for approximately forty-three miles, then turn onto the dirt Summit Lake road. Continue twelve miles then turn southwest at the fork in the road and continue two miles to the spring at Cottonwood Canyon on the southern boundary of the Sheldon National Wildlife Refuge.

From Denio Junction, the northern trailhead may be reached by following NV 140 west three miles, and then turning sharply northeast on a gravelled road. Turn again, almost immediately, to the northwest on a dirt road. If the ground is wet, this road requires a four-wheel-drive vehicle. Continue about seven miles north toward Denio Basin to the trailhead.

From Lakeview, Oregon, drive five miles north then turn east onto Oregon Highway 140. Continue eastward for approximately ninety-three miles. About three miles west-southwest of Denio Junction turn sharply northeast on a gravelled road. Turn again, almost immediately, to the northwest on a dirt road. If the ground is wet this road requires a four-wheel-drive vehicle. Continue about seven miles north toward Denio Basin to the trailhead.

The hike: The Desert Trail is not a constructed trail or a clearly defined path as are other national trails. It is a corridor through which the hiker may pass,

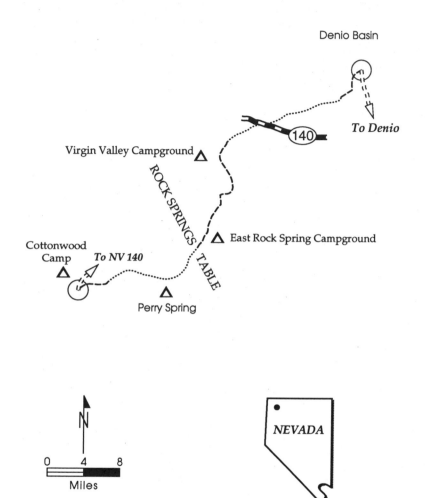

Denio Basin

To Denio

140

Virgin Valley Campground △

ROCK SPRINGS TABLE

△ East Rock Spring Campground

Cottonwood
Camp   *To NV 140*
△

△
Perry Spring

N

0   4   8
Miles

NEVADA

choosing his or her own specific route. The purpose is to avoid leaving a beaten path by minimizing the impact of the hiker on soils and vegetation. The trail follows roads and also goes cross-country. Stay on the described route to avoid private land. It is highly recommended that you have the topographic maps for navigation. Note that this section of the trail is mapped at two different scales.

Sheldon National Wildlife Refuge was set aside in 1931 for the conservation of the American pronghorn antelope. It is currently managed by the

U.S. Fish and Wildlife Service as a representative area of high desert habitat for optimum populations of all native plants and wildlife. The name of the refuge honors Charles Sheldon, who developed the wildlife refuge concept with others, early in this century.

Vegetation and habitat types include big and low sagebrush areas, and mountain mahogany and bitterbrush in the mountains above 6,000 feet. Other important habitat types include alkaline lakes, marshes, grassy spring-fed meadows, greasewood flats, juniper-covered uplands, and aspen stands in the more secluded canyons.

Bird populations vary greatly in numbers and species according to seasons. Heavy migrations of waterfowl and waterbirds visit the Sheldon Refuge during the spring and fall, with some remaining through the breeding season. During the summer months, a wide variety of smaller birds and birds of prey are present. The spring-fed riparian areas and the rock cliffs attract the summer bird populations. May to October are the best months to observe the greatest variety of bird life on the refuge. While hiking, you may see the bald eagle or the peregrine falcon, both endangered species.

Big Springs Table, a short distance north and west of the Desert Trail, provides a wintering area for up to 3,500 pronghorn antelope, which migrate to the area from as far away as Hart Mountain National Antelope Refuge, forty miles to the north.

This trail description follows the Desert Trail from south to north. The trail begins at the southern boundary of the Sheldon National Wildlife Refuge near Cottonwood Canyon. You may wish to camp and begin your hike about 1.5 miles to the north at Cottonwood Spring or at one of the two camping areas that are about 0.2 mile north of the boundary fence.

From the Refuge boundary, hike 0.25 mile north and follow the dirt road northeast and east about two miles to Bateman Spring. Continue past Bateman Spring on the road for less than a mile, then leave the road and choose your route up to the saddle north of Mahogany Mountain. Continue northeast, then east, and choose the safest route down from the saddle, which is about two miles. Hike east, staying between the steep walls of the canyon and continue on toward Alkali Flat.

You may want to take the extended trail and camp at Perry Spring. If so, hike southeast about one mile along the jeep road to Perry Spring.

Return to the trail across Alkali Flat, hike east, and carefully work your way up onto Wild Horse Pasture where you will join a jeep trail for about one mile. Leave the jeep trail and hike northeast up the slope to Rock Spring Table. Continue northeast across the relatively flat terrain for approximately three miles and descend to East Rock Spring Campground.

Leave the campground and hike northeast on the road for about eleven miles. Stay on the road in a northerly direction for another eight miles to Virgin Valley Campground. Leave the campground and hike northeast along the rim overlooking the spectacular Virgin Creek and Thousand Creek Gorge.

From the rim overlooking Thousand Creek Gorge descend to the east-northeast and hike about three miles to NV 140. Cross the highway and numerous creek beds, usually dry, and climb up the talus slope of Railroad Point. Watch for snakes and loose boulders. The view from the top is well worth the short climb. Hike north-northeast along the flat terrain and choose a safe place to descend near Black Ridge.

Hike northeast approximately six miles to the eastern boundary of Sheldon

National Wildlife Refuge. The remainder of the hike is on Bureau of Land Management land. Continue northeast for about 0.5 mile until you join a road. Hike north-northeast on the road for three to four miles to Mustang Spring and a water tank. Leave the road and hike about 1.25 miles northeast. You are now in Oregon.

Hike north about 0.4 mile, then east and northeast around the shoulder of the ridge until you join a jeep road. Follow the road northwest for about two miles to the trailhead at Denio Basin.—*Desert Trail Association*

HIKE 3 *BLUE LAKES*

General description: A day hike to a glacial lake.
General location: 67 miles north of Winnemucca.
Maps: Duffer Peak 15-minute USGS.
Difficulty: Easy.
Length: 1 mile one way.
Elevation: 7,760 to 7,968 feet.
Special attractions: Glacial lakes and topographic features, pine and aspen forest.
Water: Blue Lakes; must be purified.
Best Season: Summer through fall.
For more information: Bureau of Land Management, Winnemucca District Office, 705 East 4th St., Winnemucca, NV 89445; (702) 623-1500.
Permit: None.

Finding the trailhead: From Winnemucca drive thirty miles north on U.S. Highway 95, then forty miles west on Nevada Highway 140. Turn left on the dirt road located three-hundred yards south of the highway maintenance station, and continue seventeen miles to Onion Valley Reservoir. A high clearance vehicle is recommended. The road to Blue Lakes trailhead goes left 1.5 miles; either park at the junction or use a four-wheel drive vehicle.

The hike: The trail winds through groves of aspen and around a terminal moraine left by the ancient glacier and proceeds to Blue Lakes, a series of clear, cold lakes set in a mountain cirque. Fed by a spring and by snow melt, the five interconnected lakes are surrounded by a mixture of willow, aspen, pine, and mountain mahogany. A spur off Duffer Peak forms part of the scenic backdrop. The view from the trail yields vast panoramas that extend into California and Oregon. The lakes support a cold water fishery for trout.

Glacial moraines are distinguished from ordinary talus by the fact that they are composed of unsorted material. Glaciers collect massive amounts of rock and dirt as they slowly move down the mountain valleys, gouging their beds like giant bulldozers. Even more debris falls on the glacier from above. As the ice reaches lower elevations, it melts and drops its load of dirt, pebbles, rocks, and boulders in a jumbled, unsorted heap. This feature is clearly visible in the Blue Lakes moraines. In contrast, talus slopes form when rocks weather and fall from cliffs. Larger rocks roll farther before stopping, while small stones and pebbles tend to come to rest near the top of the slope. Likewise, rocks,

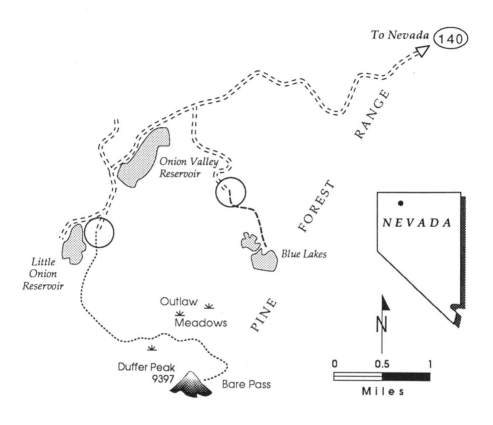

sand, and silt carried by water in streams, rivers, and floods tends to be sorted by size as it is deposited, since the carrying power of moving water decreases rapidly as the speed of the water decreases.—*Bureau of Land Management and Bruce Grubbs*

HIKE 4 *DUFFER PEAK*

General description: A cross-country day hike to the highest peak in the Pine Forest Range.
General location: 68 miles north of Winnemucca.
Maps: Duffer Peak 15-minute, Idaho Canyon 15-minute USGS.
Difficulty: Moderate.
Length: 3 miles one way.
Elevation: 7,200 to 9,397 feet.
Special attractions: Glacial topography, pine, and aspen forest.
Water: Alder Creek; should be purified.
Best season: Summer through fall.
For more information: Bureau of Land Management, Winnemucca District Office, 705 East 4th St., Winnemucca, NV 89445; (702) 623-1500.
Permit: None.

Finding the trailhead: Follow the directions for Blue Lakes (see Hike 3), but instead of taking the Blue Lakes road, continue past Onion Reservoir. At the west end of the lake, continue left over a low pass to Little Onion Reservoir. Park at the east edge of the reservoir.

The hike: The cross-country route goes through an aspen grove, skirting the east edge of Little Onion Reservoir, then follows the steep drainage of Alder Creek southeast to Outlaw Meadows. Stay on the left (north) side of this series of spacious alpine meadows past a small swampy lake, then cross the creek and head for the foot of the steep north ridge of Duffer Peak, 0.5 mile south. Pass the small but scenic Hidden Meadow and continue southeast up the steep drainage northeast of the peak. As the drainage opens out into the level expanse of Bare Pass turn right (west) and climb the steep slopes about 0.3 mile to the rugged granite ridge that forms the crown of the range.

From the summit, much of the forest for which the Pine Forest Range is named, is visible. Whitebark and limber pine, along with quaking aspen are rare in northwestern Nevada, but are abundant in this relict forest. During wetter and cooler times when glaciers were present in a few Nevada mountains and the valleys below were covered by vast lakes, trees such as these extended over a much larger area. As the climate warmed and dried, the trees and the animals that depend on them were forced higher into the mountains. In most of northwestern Nevada the pine forests simply disappeared, leaving only this tiny remnant.

Wildlife is relatively common because of the favorable habitat. Watch for deer, coyote, chukar, and sage grouse, as well as waterfowl near the lakes and reservoirs. Pronghorn, bighorn sheep, bobcat, mountain lion, beaver, badger and golden eagles are harder to spot. Also watch for birds such as the pine grosbeak and red crossbill not usually seen in this part of Nevada.

HIKE 5 *BUCKSKIN MOUNTAIN*

General description: A day hike in the Santa Rosa Range.
General location: Approximately 26 miles northeast of Orovada.
Maps: McDermitt 15-minute USGS; Humboldt National Forest (Santa Rosa Ranger District) USDAFS.
Difficulty: Moderate.
Length: 2 miles one way.
Elevation: 7,400 to 8,743 feet.
Special attractions: Colorful peak, with excellent views of the northern Santa Rosa Range.
Water: None.
Best season: Summer through fall.
For more information: Humboldt National Forest, Santa Rosa Ranger District, 1200 Winnemucca Blvd. East, Winnemucca, NV 89445; (702) 623-5025.
Permit: None.

Finding the trailhead: From Orovada, drive fourteen miles north on U.S. Highway 95, then turn right on Forest Road 084 (signed "Buckskin Canyon"). Follow the graveled dirt road east approximately twelve miles to Windy Gap; the road passes through a major wildfire burn that occurred in 1992. The pass on the crest of the Santa Rosa Range. Buckskin Mountain is the striking peak north of the road, visible from the dramatic switchbacks leading to Windy Gap. Turn north on an unmaintained road and park.

The hike: It is a moderate two-mile hike along the seldom traveled road to the summit. Stay left at the junctions. An easy alternative is to follow the main ridge crest cross-country. Watch for California bighorn sheep and mule deer in this area.

HIKE 6 *LYE CREEK BASIN*

General description: Cross country day hike in the Granite Peak area of the Santa Rosa Range.
General location: 14 miles north of Paradise Valley.
Maps: Hinkey Summit 15-minute USGS, Humboldt National Forest USDAFS.
Difficulty: Moderate.
Length: 2 miles one way.
Elevation: 7,360 to 8,800 feet.
Special attractions: Granite basin with limber pines and quaking aspen.
Water: None.
Best season: Summer through fall.
For more information: Humboldt National Forest, Santa Rosa Ranger District, 1200 E. Winnemucca Blvd., Winnemucca, NV 89445; (702) 623-5025.
Permit: None.

Finding the trailhead: From Paradise Valley, drive north on the paved Nevada Highway 792. After four miles, the pavement ends; continue straight ahead on the dirt road (FR 084) another twelve miles to Hinkey Summit, the pass at the head of Indian Creek. Continue north then turn left on Forest Road 087 to Lye Creek Campground.

The hike: Walk up the jeep road west of Lye Creek into the aspen filled basin of Lye Creek. Snowbanks continue to melt into the hot days of late August, nurturing the last flowers of summer. Cross-country hiking on game trails will bring you to small wet meadows, jumbled granite boulders, and finally, a magnificent limber pine.

During the short, crisp days of fall, brilliant red, orange, gold, and yellow aspen leaves drift silently to the ground. It is at this time of year when the mule deer bucks come out of their hiding places and can be seen with a watchful eye. Soon winter snows will put the land to sleep, and the hiker will have to wait for a new spring to awaken the buttercups and shooting stars.—
USDA Forest Service

HIKES 5, 6, & 7 *BUCKSKIN MOUNTAIN, LYE CREEK BASIN, GRANITE PEAK*

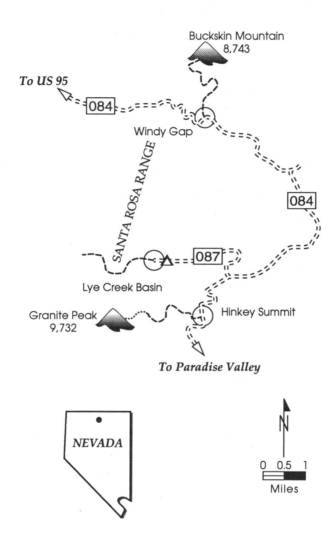

HIKE 7 *GRANITE PEAK*

General description: A cross-country day hike to the highest peak in the Santa Rosa Range.
General location: Approximately 13 miles north of Paradise Valley.
Maps: Hinkey Summit 15-minute USGS; Humboldt National Forest (Santa Rosa Ranger District) USDAFS.
Difficulty: Difficult.
Length: 3 miles one way.
Elevation: 7,800 to 9,732 feet.
Special attractions: Rugged granite peak, with excellent views of the Santa Rosa Range.
Water: None.
Best Season: Summer through fall.
For more information: Humboldt National Forest, Santa Rosa Ranger District, 1200 Winnemucca Blvd. East, Winnemucca, NV 89445; (702) 623-5025.
Permit: None.

Finding the trailhead: From Paradise Valley, drive north on the paved Nevada Highway 792. After four miles the pavement ends; continue straight ahead on the dirt road (Forest Road 084) another twelve miles to Hinkey Summit, the pass at the head of Indian Creek.

The hike: Granite Peak is visible to the west. A seldom used dirt road climbs toward the summit, passing through several stands of aspen. This road may be driven in a four-wheel drive vehicle in late summer; earlier in the season it will be impassable due to mud and snow.

The road ends in a broad sagebrush-covered saddle at a fence line. Follow the fence left (west) over a rocky section, then continue up a steep slope with excellent views of Lye Creek basin to the north. As the slope moderates, the summit is again visible. Contour around the head of a steep gully to reach the broad sagebrush saddle below the summit. Now scramble up and left to the summit.

From this airy summit, you are likely to see a golden eagle soaring on thermals as it hunts for prey. Below you in the aspen, northern goshawk and Cooper's hawk defend nesting territories. Rarely, you may see tufts of grass drying on the rocky talus slopes, left there by the elusive pika while laying in its winter food supply. Look sharp when the pika gives its short shrill warning whistle, and you may see one of the small rodents ducking out of sight in the rocks.

Even on a hot summer day, the thin mountain air is chilly. While enjoying a warm granite seat, check out the views. To the northwest, the faulted eastern face of Steens Mountain rises above the Alvord Desert in Oregon. Southeast, the Ruby Mountains still hold patches of last winter's snow. Lofty Mount Tobin is due south, and to the west, the rugged Jackson Mountains. Man and his works seem to fade to insignificance in the face of such vastness.—*Bruce Grubbs and USDA Forest Service*

HIKE 8 *REBEL CREEK TRAIL*

General description: A day hike in the Santa Rosa Range.
General location: 3 miles north of Orovada.
Maps: Hinkey Summit 15-minute USGS; Humboldt National Forest (Santa Rosa Ranger District) USDAFS.
Difficulty: Moderate.
Length: 3 miles one way.
Elevation: 5,000 to 6,800 feet.
Special attractions: Access to Santa Rosa-Paradise Peak Wilderness, with granite basin and range topography and aspen groves.
Water: Rebel Creek is not recommended for drinking.
Best season: Summer through fall.
For more information: Humboldt National Forest, Santa Rosa Ranger District, 1200 Winnemucca Blvd. East, Winnemucca, NV 89445; (702) 623-5025.
Permit: None.

Finding the trailhead: Drive three miles north of Orovada on U.S. Highway 95, and turn right at the Rebel Creek road. Continue three miles east on the dirt road, bypassing the ranch to the right (south). The road ends at the mouth of the canyon.

The hike: The foot trail is maintained and stays on the left side of the creek. After a stiff climb, the trail crosses the creek and then fades out in an aspen grove well below the main crest. It is possible to continue cross-country through the sagebrush and aspen to the crest of the Santa Rosa Range.

Cheatgrass, an introduced annual, and native grasses along with sagebrush cover the lower drainage. Willows and cottonwoods shade the stream, which supports brook and rainbow trout. Chukars are common game birds found in this environment. In the spring, buttercups, bluebells, and yellowbells bloom first, followed by lupine, skyrockets, and sunflowers, which bloom until late July. Rattlesnakes can be found in this warmer climate also.

In the higher country, mountain mahogany, aspen, serviceberry, and snowberry are common. Yellow violets, monkshood and red columbine are found in the shade of aspen groves. Mountain and western bluebirds can be seen along with many raptors. Mule deer make their summer home in the high basins and draws.

The geology changes from phyllite to granite as you move to the high country. Phyllite is a fine grained greenish gray metamorphic rock similiar to slate but often having a wavy surface and a luster due to small flecks of imbedded mica. Granite, in contrast, is a light colored metamorphic rock with a coarse, granular structure. Santa Rosa Peak at 9,701 feet is the dominant feature of the basin. The nearly vertical rim is crescent shaped with wind swept limber pine growing at the tree line. This peak lends its name to the nearby Santa Rosa-Paradise Peak Wilderness.

In the Rebel Creek drainage, the effects of heavy use by domestic stock, mainly cattle, are evident. At best, the sage rangeland can support only small numbers of cattle, and the animals naturally congregate near water sources. They form strong competition for grazing wildlife.—*Bureau of Land Management and Bruce Grubbs*

HIKES 8, 9, 10, 11, 12, 13, & 14

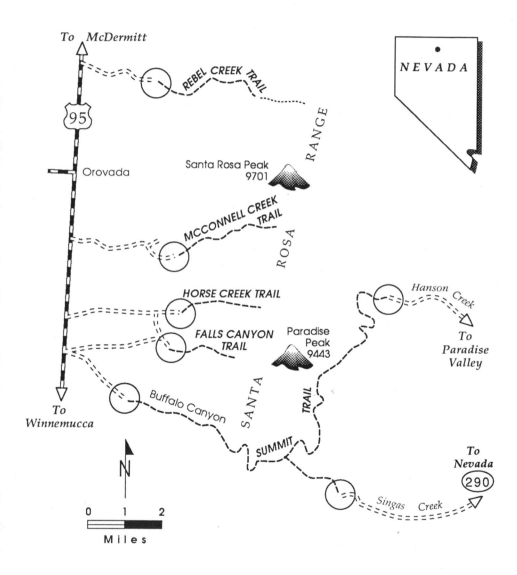

HIKE 9 *McCONNELL CREEK TRAIL*

General description: A short day hike in the Santa Rosa Range.
General location: 40 miles north of Winnemucca.
Maps: Hinkey Summit 15-minute USGS; Humboldt National Forest (Santa Rosa Ranger District) USDAFS.
Difficulty: Moderate.
Length: 3 miles one way.
Elevation: 5,000 to 6,800 feet.
Special attractions: Access to Santa Rosa-Paradise Peak Wilderness, and granite, and phyllite geology, with open views of Santa Rosa Peak.
Water: McConnell Creek is not recommended for drinking.
Best season: Summer through fall.
For more information: Humboldt National Forest, Santa Rosa Ranger District, 1200 Winnemucca Blvd. East, Winnemucca, NV 89445; (702) 623-5025.
Permit: None.

Finding the trailhead: Drive forty miles north of Winnemucca on U.S. Highway 95, and turn right at the McConnell Creek Road. Continue three miles east of the highway. The trailhead is a hundred yards inside the USDA Forest Service boundary fence on the northeast side of the creek.

The hike: Minimal trail maintenance is done at the beginning of the season. The upper basin is wide with a view of Santa Rosa Peak, the striking granite peak that dominates the southern part of the range.

Phyllite outcrops and grassy hillsides greet the hiker in the lower portion of the drainage. Access to the creek is difficult due to a deeply cut channel, but brook trout can be caught if the fisherman is persistent. A sharp eye might catch a glimpse of the California bighorn sheep that inhabit the area to the north. A lack of trees gives an open feeling to the lower canyon.

The geology changes midway up the canyon to granite ridges and soil made up of decomposed granite. Golden eagles soar on the air currents and small lizards watch from their sunny perches on the rocks. Aspen, mountain mahogany, and snowberry begin to fill the draws and slopes. Willows grow along the drainages. As you enter McConnell Basin, there is a stunning view of the steep and rocky west slope of Santa Rosa Peak.—*Bureau of Land Management*

HIKE 10 *HORSE CANYON TRAIL*

General description: A short day hike in the Santa Rosa Range.
General location: 38 miles north of Winnemucca.
Maps: Hinkey Summit 15-minute, Paradise Valley 15-minute USGS; Humboldt National Forest (Santa Rosa Ranger District) USFS.
Difficulty: Moderate.
Length: 2 miles one way.
Elevation: 5,000 to 6,500 feet.
Special attractions: Access to Santa Rosa-Paradise Peak Wilderness, and basalt-granite geology.
Water: Horse Creek is not recommended for drinking.
Best season: Summer through fall.
For more information: Humboldt National Forest, Santa Rosa Ranger District, 1200 E. Winnemucca Blvd., Winnemucca, NV 89445; (702) 623-5025.
Permit: None.

Finding the trailhead: Drive thirty-eight miles north of Winnemucca on U.S. Highway 95, and turn right at the Horse Canyon Road (signed). Vehicles with high clearance are recommended to reach this trailhead, which is 3.5 miles east of the highway. The actual trailhead is a hundred-fifty yards southeast inside the USDA Forest Service boundary fence. From here, the trail follows the creek, becoming a cattle trail near the end.

The hike: Record snow accumulated on the Santa Rosa Mountains in the winter of 1983-1984. In late May, a sudden change of temperature from freezing to over ninety degrees caused rapid snowmelt. The ground became saturated with water and the creeks rose. Within twenty-four hours of the abrupt temperature change, midslides containing massive amounts of debris and torrents of water gutted several streams. Damage caused by that hundred-year flood event is still evident today in the form of steeply cut banks, mudslide scars and high water debris. The skeletal remains of aspen and old cotton-wood trees are now home to birds and small animals.

The granite-rimmed skyline rings the basin. While sitting under a mountain mahogany in the cool breeze, you can view a wide variety of vegetation. Quaking apsen, alder, and limber pine occur on the north facing slopes, which hold snow longer. Mountain mahogany, serviceberry, snowberry, and sagebrush occur on the sun dried south facing slopes. House wrens, red-shafted flickers, and mountain chickadees call from the trees. Inconspicuous Jacob's ladder, penstemon, and clarkia flowers grow amongst the rocks.—*USDA Forest Service*

HIKE 11 *FALLS CANYON TRAIL*

General description: A short day hike in the Santa Rosa Range.
General location: 38 miles north of Winnemucca.
Maps: Hinkey Summit 15-minute, Paradise Valley 15-minute USGS; Humboldt National Forest (Santa Rosa Ranger District) USFS.
Difficulty: Moderate.
Length: 1.5 miles one way.
Elevation: 5,000 to 6,000 feet.
Special attractions: Access to the Santa Rosa-Paradise Peak Wilderness, and a waterfall.
Water: Falls Creek is not recommended for drinking.
Best season: Summer through fall.
For more information: Humboldt National Forest, Santa Rosa Ranger District, 1200 E. Winnemucca Blvd., Winnemucca, NV 89445; (702) 623-5025.
Permit: None.

Finding the trailhead: Drive thirty-eight miles north of Winnemucca on U.S. Highway 95, and turn right at the Horse Canyon Road (signed). Vehicles with high clearance are recommended to reach this trailhead, which is 3.5 miles east of the highway. The actual trailhead is a hundred yards northeast inside the USDA Forest Service boundary fence.

The hike: Generally, the trail stays along the creek until you get into the upper basin. Minimal trail maintenance is done at the beginning of the season.

Just after entering the canyon, you'll come to the waterfall that gives the canyon its name. It is small, but when the water is flowing wildly during the spring snowmelt or is frozen in hanging needles of ice in the winter, it can be a beautiful sight. The vertical walls of phyllite to the south at the canyon entrance are awe inspiring. Granite features take over a short distance up the canyon. A lone limber pine grows out of a fissure in a single granite boulder in the sagebrush basin. Robins love the choke cherries in the fall when the fruit is ripe. Choke cherries as well as elder berries can be picked and made into jelly, syrup, and wine.

Occurring in fairly widespread stands in the Santa Rosa Range, the quaking aspen is North America's most widely distributed tree. It grows throughout the western mountains at elevations between the pine belt and the spruce-fir belt. In the Santa Rosa Range where the alpine forests are conspicuously absent, aspen is the major tree, sharing the slopes with a few limber pine. In the fall, the leaves turn a brilliant yellow with patches of orange and red, brightening entire mountain sides. The name quaking aspen refers to the fact that the leaves, attached by thin flat stems, tremble in the lightest breeze.— *USDA Forest Service and Bruce Grubbs*

The falls in Falls Canyon, Santa Rosa Range. USDA Forest Service photo.

HIKE 12 SANTA ROSA SUMMIT TRAIL—BUFFALO CANYON

General description: A day hike in the Santa Rosa Range.
General location: 35 miles north of Winnemucca.
Maps: Five Fingers 7.5-minute, Paradise Peak 15-minute, Hinkey Summit 15-minute USGS; Humboldt National Forest (Santa Rosa Ranger District) USDAFA.
Difficulty: Difficult.
Length: 4.5 miles one way.
Elevation: 4,400 to 8,200 feet.
Special attractions: Access to the Santa Rosa-Paradise Peak Wilderness, panoramic views.
Water: Avoid drinking from streams and springs because of giardia.
Best season: Summer and fall.
For more information: Humboldt National Forest, Santa Rosa Ranger District, 1200 E. Winnemucca Blvd., Winnemucca, NV 89445; (702) 623-5025.
Permit: None.

Finding the trailhead: From Winnemucca, drive thirty-five miles north on U.S. Highway 95, then turn right at the Buffalo Canyon road sign. Follow the dirt road two miles. The trail begins northwest of the USDA Forest Service boundary fence.

The hike: The first half of the trail to the crest was constructed in 1986, and passes through sagebrush, various grasses, willows, and cottonwoods. The upper half is older and more primitive and passes through snowberry, serviceberry, mahogany, and aspen. A steep climb to the crest completes the last half mile.

For access to the trail on the east side of the range see Hike 13 Santa Rosa Summit Trail—Singas Creek and Hike 14 Santa Rosa Summit Trail—North Hanson Creek.

The trail crosses Buffalo Canyon Creek several times during its journey to the summit at 8,000 feet. Passage in the lower part of the drainage is via a trail constructed around phyllite outcrops and narrow benches. The harsh weather conditions of the mountain country have molded the channel of Buffalo Creek. Severe thunderstorms are hazardous to both the environment and man. Be prepared for sudden changes in the weather.

Mountain lions are known to travel throughout the drainage. Mule deer can be seen browsing on the snowberry and aspen saplings in the high basins. The fall colors of the aspen and snowberry are brilliant gold, orange, yellow, and red. Rabbitbrush and sagebrush are late bloomers that display yellow flowers.

The view to the east from the summit of Buffalo Canyon includes Paradise Valley dotted with ranches and farms, and the Snowstorm and Independence Mountains of Elko County. The Jackson and Pine Forest ranges are to the west. A trail south along the crest affords more panoramic views.

The lower sage covered slopes of the Santa Rosa Range are pronghorn country. Averaging about 4 feet long and 90 to 125 pounds, the pronghorn are distinguished by the forward projecting prong on their horns. When alarmed, they raise the white fur of their rump patch as a signal to the other members of their band, and can run at speeds of forty to fifty miles per hour through the open sage and grassland. The pronghorn have developed an interesting adaptation to the temperature extremes of the high desert. The thick tubular fur contains large air cells, and each hair can be raised or lowered. In cold weather, the heavy fur is held close to the body, providing maximum insulation and wind protection, and in summer the raised hairs allow more air circulation and cooling of the skin.—*USDA Forest Service and Bruce Grubbs*

HIKE 13 *SANTA ROSA SUMMIT TRAIL— SINGAS CREEK*

General description: Day hikes and access to the southern portion of the Summit Trail.
General location: 42 miles northeast of Winnemucca.
Maps: Five Fingers 7.5-minute, Paradise Peak 15-minute, USGS; Humboldt National Forest (Santa Rosa Ranger District) USDAFS.
Difficulty: Moderate.
Length: 0.5 mile minimum one way.
Elevation: 6,500 to 7,300 feet.
Special attractions: Singas Trailhead with ample parking, and a major access point for the Santa Rosa-Paradise Peak Wilderness.
Water: Avoid drinking from perennial streams due to giardia.
Best season: Summer and fall.
For more information: Humboldt National Forest, Santa Rosa Ranger District, 1200 E. Winnemucca Blvd., Winnemucca, NV 89445; (702) 623-5025.
Permit: None.

Finding the trailhead: From Winnemucca, go twenty-two miles north on U.S. Highway 95, then turn right on Nevada Highway 290 and continue seventeen miles to the signed Singas Creek Road. Turn left and drive five miles to the parking area (a high clearance vehicle is necessary).

The hike: From the parking area, it is a steep half-mile climb along an old road to the Summit Trail, which can be hiked south or north from Singas Basin. This hike covers the trail to the saddle at the head of Buffalo Canyon. Other sections of the Summit Trail are covered under two other hike descriptions: Santa Rosa Summit Trail—North Hanson Creek, and Santa Rosa Summit Trail—Buffalo Canyon.

After the initial climb, the trail goes south across the hillside toward a saddle and descends slightly as it crosses the head of Morey Creek. After contouring through the head of Abel Creek, the Summit Trail climbs southwest over a point on the ridge south of Abel Creek. A final steep climb across the slope to the west leads to the main crest of the Santa Rosa Range at the head of Buffalo Canyon.

Hidden from view by foothills, the Singas Creek Basin is filled with aspen and streams fed by the spring snowmelt from surrounding peaks with steep granite faces. Views are spectacular from either direction on the Summit Trail.

Marmots, a large alpine rodent, chirp a warning before disappearing into their rock dens. Patience may be rewarded when a curious marmot pops his head back out to get a look at the intruder. You may see a downy woodpecker, which nests in cavities. House wrens and Wilson's warbler flit among the willows and aspen trees. Early morning and late evening are the mule deer's favorite time for browsing. Tall, flowering bluebells, larkspur, and jewel flower can be found most of the summer. The fragile blue flax and hardy mountain iris favor wet meadows.—*USDA Forest Service and Bruce Grubbs*

HIKE 14 *SANTA ROSA SUMMIT TRAIL— NORTH HANSON CREEK*

General description: Day hikes and access to the Summit Trail.
General location: 44 miles northeast of Winnemucca.
Maps: Paradise Peak 15-minute, Hinkey Summit 15-minute USGS; Humboldt National Forest (Santa Rosa Ranger District) USDAFS.
Difficulty: Easy.
Length: Various.
Elevation: 6,000 to 6,400 feet.
Special attractions: Closest vehicle access to the Summit Trail, and access to the Santa Rosa-Paradise Peak Wilderness.
Water: Avoid drinking from perennial streams due to giardia.
Best season: Summer and fall.
For more information: Humboldt National Forest, Santa Rosa Ranger District, 1200 E. Winnemucca Blvd., Winnemucca, NV 89445; (702) 623-5025.
Permit: None.

Finding the trailhead: From Winnemucca, go twenty-two miles north on U.S. Highway 95, then turn right on Nevada Highway 290 and continue eighteen miles to Paradise Valley. Turn right at the main intersection and drive 1.5 miles to the end of the road. Turn left (south) and continue for 0.5 mile. Then turn right on the dirt road that follows the fence line to the west. Continue up into the foothills until you reach a fork in the road. Here you cross the creek and continue west up into the basin. The trail is just west of the parking area. A high clearance vehicle should be used to reach this trail.

The hike: The Summit Trail can be hiked south or north from the North Hanson Creek trailhead. This access affords the hiker several options: a hike to the south to the Singas Creek Trailhead, or a more primitive hike to the north on a less well defined tail. Either trail provides an easy hike.

This hike describes the section to the south. The trail climbs the hillside to the southwest, then passes through a saddle after about 0.5 miles and climbs gradually along the sage-covered hillside. Another short steep section leads through a saddle at 7,000 feet, then the Summit Trail drops into Singas Creek. It is approximately 0.5 mile to the Singas Creek road, visible below. For information on the Summit Trail south of Singas Creek, see Hike 13 description.

Limber pines dot the granite basins high above the trail. North Hanson and Lamance drainages meld together to form one large basin. Willows, aspen, snowberry, and blue Forget-me-Not greet the hiker. Red tailed hawks perch in aspen and the noisy raven is common.—*USDA Forest Service and Bruce Grubbs*

HIKE 15 *WATER CANYON*

General description: A day hike in the Sonoma Range.
General location: 5 miles south of Winnemucca.
Maps: Winnemucca East 7.5-minute, Sonoma Canyon 7.5-minute, Adelaide 7.5-minute, Pole Creek 7.5-minute USGS.
Difficulty: Difficult.
Length: 8-mile loop.
Elevation: 5,900 to 8,900 feet.
Special attractions: Views of the historic Humboldt River valley.
Water: None.
Best season: Summer and fall.
Form more information: Bureau of Land Management, Winnemucca District Office, 705 E. 4th St., Winnemucca, NV 89445; (702) 623-1500.
Permit: None.

Finding the trailhead: From downtown Winnemucca at the junction of business Interstate 80 and U.S. Highway 95, drive east one block, then turn right and continue about one mile to the end of the street. Turn right, and then go left at the edge of town on the dirt road to Water Canyon. Continue about five miles to the end of the road at an aspen grove.

The hike: On the left, a jeep road switchbacks steeply up the slope. Either walk up the road or go directly up the slope to the right of the road. Both routes lead to the top of the ridge northeast of Water Canyon. Follow the jeep road and the ridge southeast around the head of Water Canyon to the high point about three miles north of Sonoma Peak. Also, it is possible to detour south to the peak; this would add about six miles to the hike.

From the high point, hike cross-country along the ridge west and northwest above Water Canyon about one mile, then drop down the ridge north to reach the creek about a mile upstream of the parking area. An old road leads down the creek to the parking area.

During the walk along the high ridges, a large portion of the Humboldt River valley is visible. The Humboldt is Nevada's longest river but never reaches the sea, in keeping with the character of the Great Basin. It rises near the town of Wells in northeastern Nevada and crosses northern Nevada to the west and then south to finally disappear in the alkaline flats of the Humboldt Sink. Although it covers only 280 air miles, it has a very low gradient and meanders so much that the river channel is actually 1,000 miles long. The Humboldt River valley was a major emigrant trail during the settling of California and Oregon; the ill-fated Donner party passed this way.

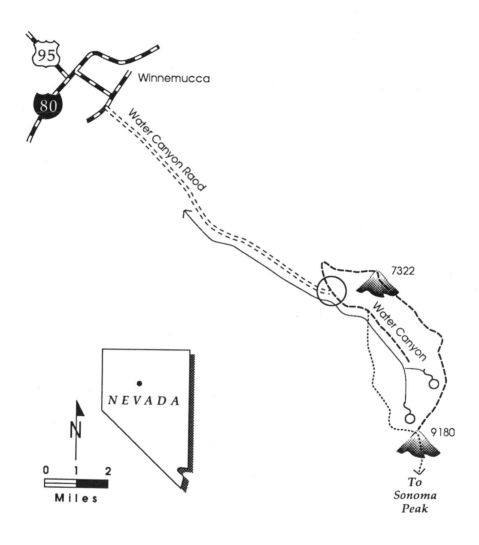

HIKE 16 *STAR PEAK*

General description: A day hike to the highest peak in the Humboldt Range.
General location: Approximately 56 miles southwest of Winnemucca.
Maps: Star Peak 7.5-minute USGS.
Difficulty: Difficult.
Length: 4 miles one way.
Elevation: 5,700 to 9,836 feet.
Special attractions: Expansive views.
Water: None.
Best season: Summer through fall.
For more information: Bureau of Land Management, Winnemucca District Office, 705 E. 4th St., Winnemucca, NV 89445; (702) 623-1500.
Permit: None.

Finding the trailhead: From Winnemucca, drive about forty-six miles west on Interstate 80 and exit at the Humboldt interchange. Follow the dirt road south along the east side of the freeway approximately 4.5 miles, then turn east toward Star Peak (the highest point in the East Humboldt Range) and drive three miles into Eldorado Canyon. After crossing the creek several times, the road veers left and climbs steeply out of the creek. Park here unless you have a four-wheel drive vehicle.

The hike: It's a steep hike up the road through the juniper forest, but the reward is an ever-expanding view. After about 1.5 miles, the road follows the ridge top east and climbs less steeply. About three miles from Eldorado Creek the road turns left (north) along the slopes of Star Peak. Leave the road and go directly up the west ridge to the summit, or continue along the road north until it reaches the summit ridge, then walk south up the ridge to Star Peak. There are hundred-mile views in all directions, and the view of the Humboldt River valley and Rye Patch Reservoir are especially fine.

The pygmy forest of juniper trees on the lower slopes of the Humboldt Range is almost startling to the hiker who has spent time in the ranges of northwestern Nevada. There are few trees on most of the ranges from the vicinity of Winnemucca northward and westward, the exceptions being a few junipers on the lower slopes, and a few aspens on the higher slopes. In comparison, ranges with similar elevations in eastern Nevada support varied forests. Probably the lack of trees is caused by the Sierra Nevada and Cascade Mountains to the west, which intercept much of the moisture from winter storms. Also, little moisture in the form of summer thunderstorms reaches northwestern Nevada. But farther to the southeast, closer to the source of tropical moisture, there are more summer rains and more trees on the mountains.

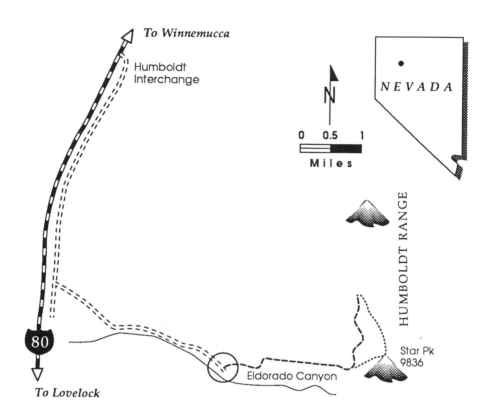

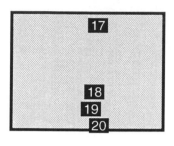

17. Matterhorn Peak
18. Ruby Crest National Recreation Trail
19. Echo Lake
20. Overland Lake Loop

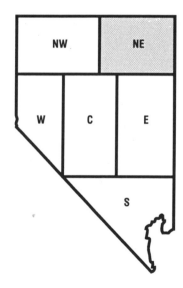

HIKE 17 *MATTERHORN PEAK*

General description: A two- or three-day backpack trip over the major peaks of the Jarbidge Crest.

General location: Approximately 105 miles north of Elko.

Maps: Jarbidge South 7.5-minute, Gods Pocket Peak 7.5-minute USGS, Humboldt National Forest (Jarbidge Ranger District) USDAFS.

Difficulty: Difficult.

Length: 12-mile loop.

Elevation: 6,945 to 10,839 feet.

Special attractions: Spectacular views from the highest peaks of the range.

Water: Upper Jarbidge River, Jarbidge Lake.

Best season: Summer through fall.

For more information: Humboldt National Forest, Jarbidge Ranger District, 1008 Burley Ave, Buhl, ID 83316-1812; (208) 543-4129.

Permit: None.

Finding the trailhead: The Jarbidge Mountains in extreme northeastern Nevada are located in Nevada's first Wilderness Area. Remote and time-consuming to reach, they are well worth the effort. From Twin Falls, Idaho, go south on U.S. Highway 93 for approximately twenty-eight miles to Rogerson, Idaho. Take the signed turnoff for Jarbidge and follow this road seventy miles (the first fifty miles are paved, the rest unpaved) to the trailhead at the end of the road at Snowslide Gulch.

From Elko, go north on Nevada Highway 225 for seventy-three miles to the signed turnoff for Jarbidge. Twenty-six miles after leaving the pavement turn right and continue four miles to the end of the road at Snowslide Gulch.

The hike: The Jarbidge River Trail starts out as an old road and becomes a foot trail as it climbs up the canyon. The forest is open, and there are excellent views. Part way up, an old trail is visible as it branches to the right into an area of avalanche debris.

The amount of destruction caused by snow avalanches can be awesome. In remote areas such as this, they are only a hazard to backcountry travelers. But in developed areas such as ski areas or mining camps, they can be very destructive. Several mining camps in the western mountains of the United States were destroyed by avalanches in the last century. Avalanches tend to recur on the same slopes so that the location of avalanche paths can be mapped by examining the growth pattern of trees. Often an avalanche path will have a central area that is bare of all but grass and low brush. This indicates that avalanches occur often enough to keep trees from growing, at least every few years and possibly every year. On the fringes of the avalanche path there may be a uniform growth of short, young trees. The age of these trees shows the time, possibly fifty years, that has elapsed since the last avalanche large enough to sweep the entire path. Less obvious may be the possibility that the much older trees to either side of the young trees may also be uniform in age, even though they are two hundred years or more in age. This means that periodic oversize avalanches also occur, though perhaps only every two hundred to three hundred years.

Matterhorn Peak in the Jarbidge Mountains looking south from Jarbidge Peak. This photo shows most of the crest traverse. USDA Forest Service photo.

There is good camping in the vicinity of Jarbidge Lake (really a pond). Switchbacks lead up to the crest south of the lake, where a signed trail descends south into the Mary's River country. Continue up more switchbacks to the pass between Mary's River Peak and Cougar Peak. This is a good goal for a day hike.

The strenuous and difficult crest traverse begins by crossing Cougar Peak, which is relatively easy. To the north, the ridge is narrow with a 250-foot cliff and bristlecone pines crowding the narrow crest.

Matterhorn Peak looks steep but is easy to climb when dry (it would be dangerous if the route was snow covered). Of course the views are excellent in all directions, and the view down the precipitous north face is dizzying. North of Matterhorn Peak the ridge becomes easier. There is some limited camping in the saddles, but the only water source is snow, if available. It is possible to continue north to Jarbidge Peak, the last high peak in the range, which has fine views north into Idaho.

Return to the trailhead by descending the steep west ridge of Jumbo Peak. This route is straightforward until about 1,000 feet above the trailhead. Here a flat terminates in steep cliffs, which can be bypassed by dropping south into Snowslide Gulch. The worst of the brush can be avoided by means of deer trails.

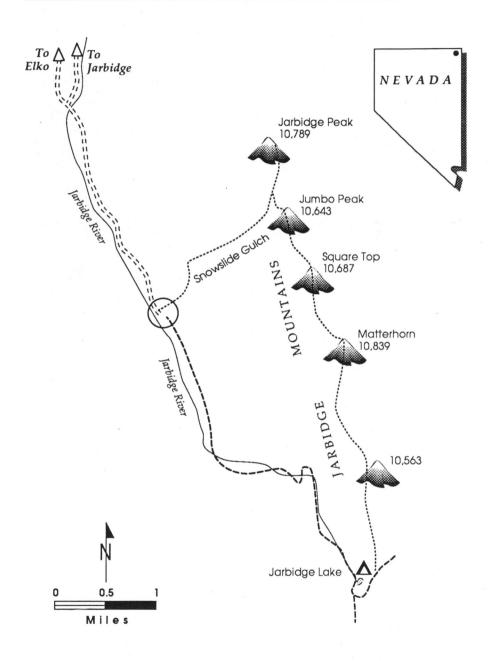

To Elko

To Jarbidge

NEVADA

Jarbidge River

Jarbidge Peak
10,789

Jumbo Peak
10,643

Snowslide Gulch

Square Top
10,687

MOUNTAINS

Matterhorn
10,839

Jarbidge River

JARBIDGE

10,563

N

0   0.5   1
Miles

Jarbidge Lake

The north trailhead for the Ruby Crest Trail is easily reached via a good paved road up spectacular Lamoille Canyon. Several Forest Service campgrounds make it easy to camp before starting the hike.

HIKE 18 *RUBY CREST NATIONAL RECREATION TRAIL*

General description: A four-day backpack trip in the Ruby Mountains.
General location: 42 miles south of Elko.
Maps: Lamoille 15-minute, Green Mountain 7.5-minute, Franklin Lake NW 7.5-minute, Franklin Lake SW 7.5-minute, Harrison Pass 7.5-minute USGS, Humboldt National Forest (Ruby Mountains Ranger District) USDAFS.
Difficulty: Difficult.
Length: About 37 miles one way.
Elevation: 7,247 to 10,893 feet.
Special attractions: Classic alpine scenery, glacial valleys, cirques, and mountain lakes and streams.
Water: Plentiful in lakes and streams north of Overland Lake; somewhat drier the last 12 miles to Harrison Pass.
Best season: Late summer through fall.
For more information: Humboldt National Forest, Ruby Mountains Ranger District, P.O. Box 246, Wells, NV 89825; (702) 752-3357.
Permit: None.

Finding the trailhead: From Elko, drive south on Nevada Highway 228 and turn left on Nevaday Highway 277. Just before the hamlet of Lamoille, turn right on the paved Lamoille Canyon Road (signed). Continue to the parking loop at the end of the road.

If the complete Crest Trail is hiked one way, a vehicle should be left at Harrison Pass, which is reached from Elko via NV 228. Continue past Jiggs, where the pavement ends, on the good dirt road to a junction. Turn left (east) on the signed Harrison Pass road and continue to Harrison Pass. The Ruby Crest Trail begins as a jeep road winding north along the crest.

The hike: This popular and scenic trail follows the approximate crest of the Ruby Mountains from the end of the Lamoille Canyon Road about thirty-seven miles to Harrison Pass. All of the trail may be hiked one-way as a four or five day backpack trip, or either end may be walked as day hikes of various lengths.

Lamoille Canyon displays the classic U-shaped profile of a glacier-carved alpine valley. USDA Forest Service interpretive displays along the road point out the distinctive features of the canyon. Numerous avalanche paths descend the steep walls; some years the road is blocked by a tangled mixture of trees and rock-hard snow brought down by the avalanches. The Ruby Mountains are the most alpine of Nevada ranges, with rugged granite peaks and crystal lakes.

From the trailhead, the trail climbs past Lamoille Lake over Liberty Pass, then descends past Liberty Lake to Favre Lake. After passing the turnoff to North Furlong Lake, the last of the series of glacial lakes, the trail reaches its highest point at Wines Peak. To the south of Wines Peak, the trail follows the general crest until it drops into the Overland Creek drainage and contours to Overland Lake. Above the lake the trail climbs steeply over the crest into the North Fork Smith Creek and stays well west of the crest as it heads into the west side canyons, only regaining the crest about two miles north of Harrison Pass.

HIKES **18 & 19** *RUBY CREST TRAIL, ECHO LAKE*

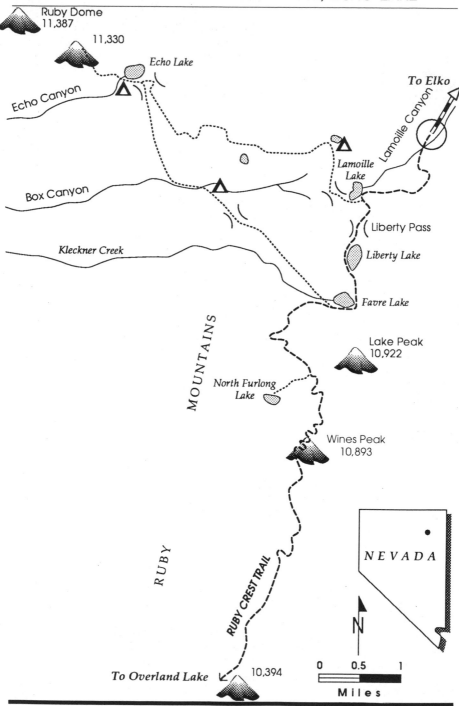

Ruby Dome
11,387

11,330

Echo Lake

Echo Canyon

To Elko

Lamoille Canyon

Lamoille Lake

Box Canyon

Liberty Pass

Kleckner Creek

Liberty Lake

Favre Lake

Lake Peak
10,922

M O U N T A I N S

North Furlong Lake

Wines Peak
10,893

R U B Y

RUBY CREST TRAIL

To Overland Lake

10,394

NEVADA

N

0   0.5   1

M i l e s

The northern section of the Ruby Mountains contain more glacial lakes than any other range in Nevada. These lakes are the main reason the mountains appear so alpine. The lakes formed after the glaciers melted and runoff water filled the depressions left behind. Glaciers tend to form depressions in their beds in two ways; by bulldozing rocks into a dam (known as a terminal moraine), or by carving out basins in the bedrock (called grinding down at the heel).

HIKE 19 *ECHO LAKE*

General description: A two- or three-day backpack trip in the Ruby Mountains.
General location: 42 miles south of Elko.
Maps: Lamoille 15-minute USGS, Humboldt National Forest (Ruby Mountains Ranger District) USDAFS.
Difficulty: Difficult.
Length: 13-mile loop.
Elevation: 8,800 to 10,880 feet
Special attractions: Scenic, lesser traveled area of the popular Ruby Mountains.
Water: Dollar, Lamoille, Echo, Favre, and Liberty Lakes; Box, Kleckner, and Lamoille Creeks.
Best season: Late summer through fall.
For more information: Humboldt National Forest, Ruby Mountains Ranger District, P.O. Box 246, Wells, NV 89825; (702) 752-3357.
Permit: None.

Finding the trailhead: From Elko, drive south on Nevada Highway 228 and turn left on Nevada Highway 277. Just before the hamlet of Lamoille, turn right on the paved Lamoille Canyon Road (signed). Continue to the parking loop at the end of the road.

The hike: Follow the Ruby Crest Trail to Lamoille Lake, then leave the trail and skirt the lake on either side and climb to the saddle at the head of Box Canyon. Now contour to the right around the head of Box Canyon and generally work east to the saddle south of Echo Lake. This traverse is strenuous, but the fine views and the two small, unnamed hanging lakes are worth it. It is probably easier to descend into Box Canyon and climb up the side drainage to the saddle south of Echo Lake. From this saddle drop down to the lake; there are campsites in the trees near the outlet.

An optional side hike to the west, heading a cirque, leads to an 11,330-foot ridge and an excellent view of Ruby Dome, the highest peak in the range.

From Echo Lake climb back to the saddle south of the lake, then descend the scenic hanging valley to the south into Box Canyon. There are good campsites in aspens stands in the broad valley floor. About one mile east of the point where Box Creek is first reached climb south over a saddle then contour east into the head of Kleckner Creek. Some sections of the traverse are rough.

Both Kleckner and Box Canyons are very scenic, with grassy north slopes,

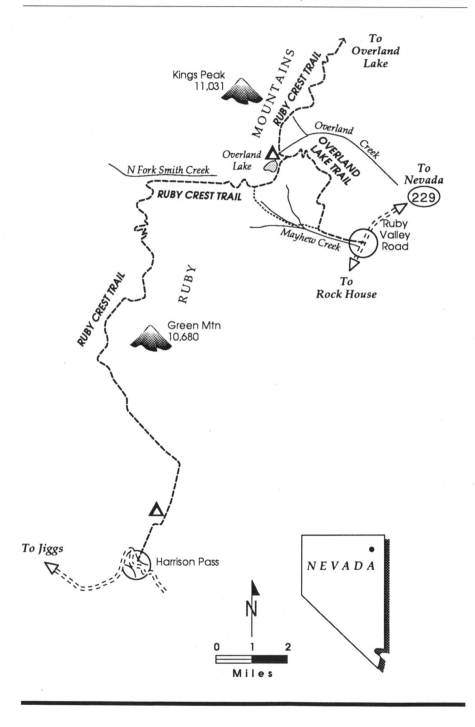

pine-forested south slopes, and aspen glades in the canyon floors. At the west end of Favre Lake, rejoin the Ruby Crest Trail.

Follow the trail east and north around Favre Lake and up to Liberty Lake, over Liberty Pass, and past Lamoille Lake to the trailhead. Glacial features such as horn shaped peaks, cirques, hanging valleys, and U-shaped valleys dominate the scenery on this rugged loop. Cirques are the birthplace of glaciers, which start to form when more snow falls than melts each year. After many layers of snow are deposited, the weight compresses the lower layers into ice, which begins to flow slowly downhill. At the heads of the valleys, the ice eats away at all three slopes. After the glacier melts, the classic bowl-shaped valley head is exposed, often containing one or more deep lakes. The mountain summits, their flanks worn away by the ice in the valleys, present sheer faces and knife edge ridges. As the ice progresses down the valleys, it carves away at the sides, converting the V-shaped valley created by water to a U-shape. Side glaciers contribute ice to the main glacier just as creeks contribute water to a river. The main glacier lowers its bed much faster than its tributaries, so that when the ice melts, hanging valleys are formed with floors much higher than the main valley. The ice also leaves behind such telltale signs as moraines and polished rock slabs with scratches showing the direction the ice moved.

HIKE 20 *OVERLAND LAKE LOOP*

General description: A day hike or two-day backpack trip in the Ruby Mountains.
General location: About 60 miles southeast of Elko.
Maps: Franklin Lake NW 7.5-minute USGS, Humboldt National Forest (Ruby Mountains Ranger District) USDAFS.
Difficulty: Difficult.
Length: 14-mile loop.
Elevation: 6,120 to 10,160 feet.
Special attractions: Alpine lake and scenery, superb views of the Ruby Valley.
Water: Mayhew Creek and Overland Lake.
Best season: Late summer through fall.
For more information: Humboldt National Forest, Ruby Mountains Ranger District, P.O. Box 246, Wells, NV 89825; (702) 752-3357.
Permit: None.

Finding the trailhead: Access to the spectacular east side of the Ruby Mountains is difficult due to the private land along the foothills. Overland Lake is an exception, being reachable by USDA Forest Service trail.

From Elko drive east on Interstate 80 for twenty miles, then right (southeast) on Nevada Highway 229 over Secret Pass. The paved road continues south along the east side of the range for several miles, then abruptly turns northeast at a junction. Continue south on the dirt Ruby Valley road approximately seventeen miles and park at the jeep trail shown on the topographic map just north of Mayhew Creek, about a mile north of Rock House.

The hike: Do not follow the jeep trail. The Overland Lake Trail follows the fence, crosses the small drainage, and again follows the fence. This section is confused by numerous cattle trails. At the section corner where the topographic map shows the elevation of 6,278 feet, another trail comes through a gate from the left (south). Above this point, the trail is more distinct. Stay on the trail about one mile; when the trail turns right and starts away from the creek and up the slope drop down and cross the nameless north fork of Mayhew Creek as well as the main creek. These crossings are brushy, but the walking is better on the far side. Follow the ridge just south of the main creek all the way to the crest. Hike north along the ridge less than 0.2 miles to join the Ruby Crest Trail.

The trail climbs about 300 feet to a saddle then descends steeply to Overland Lake, which is perched in a scenic glacial cirque. Follow the trail around the east side of the lake and then down the steep forested slopes below the lake about 0.3 miles to the junction with the Overland Lake Trail. Turn right (east) and continue as the trail crosses the south slopes of Overland Canyon then works its way south into the Mayhew Creek drainage. A one mile descent leads to Mayhew Creek and the point where the trail was left.

WESTERN NEVADA

21. Hobart Reservoir
22. Spooner Lake
23. Marlette Lake
24. Jones Creek—Whites Creek Trail
25. Mount Rose
26. Ophir Creek Trail
27. Grimes Point Archaeological Area
28. Sand Springs Desert Study Area

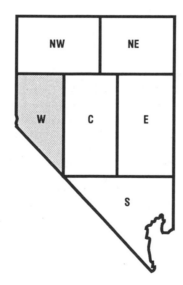

HIKE 21 HOBART RESERVOIR

General description: A day hike or overnight backpack trip in the Carson Range.

General location: 21 miles west of Carson City.

Maps: Marlette Lake 7.5-minute, Carson City 7.5-minute USGS, Toiyabe National Forest (Carson Ranger District) USDAFS.

Difficulty: Difficult.

Length: 7 miles one way.

Elevation: 6,400 to 8,000 feet.

Special attractions: Historic water system.

Water: Franktown Creek designated camp site.

Best season: Summer through fall.

For more information: Nevada Division of State Parks, 1060 Mallory Way, Carson City, NV 89701; (702) 885-4379.

Permit: None. Camping permitted only in the two designated sites in the backcountry.

Finding the trailhead: From Carson City drive south on U.S. Highway 395 three miles then turn west on U.S. Highway 50. Continue ten miles then turn north on Nevada Highway 28. The trailhead is at Hidden Beach, eight miles from US 50. Parking is very limited.

The hike: This trail climbs from the shore of Lake Tahoe about 1.5 miles to Tunnel Creek station, a maintenance station on the Marlette water system. This water system transported lumber as well as valuable water to Virginia City during the mining period. Flume lines, originating at Marlette Lake and Mill Creek, carried water and wood to the western portal of this 4,000 foot tunnel through the Carson Range. At the eastern portal, the flumes then connected to the Hobart Creek water system. Some of the flume lines are still visible.

The trail continues over an 8,000-foot pass, where short side trails lead to Twin Lakes. The main trail continues about one mile down to Franktown Creek, a designated camp site. The trail continues another mile to Red House, which was occupied by the Marlette water system flume tenders. This was the site of the first diversion dam on Hobart Creek, a project that marked the beginning of the use of Sierra Nevada water for the Virginia City mines. This was a revolutionary engineering feat for the times. The original Red House was built in 1887 but was washed away in a flood during 1907. The present building was built about 1910 and was used until the late 1950s.

Continuing up Hobart Creek, the trail reaches Hobart Reservoir in about another mile. The dam was constructed in 1887 to add extra capability to the Marlette water system. It is now the sole water source for Virginia City, Silver City, and Gold Hill. It also supplies parts of Carson City and Lakeview. It is popular for fishing although strictly regulated (only artificial lures can be used).—*Nevada Division of Parks*

HIKE 22 *SPOONER LAKE*

General description: A day hike in the Carson Range.
General location: 13 miles west of Carson City.
Maps: Glenbrook 7.5-minute USGS, Toiyabe National Forest (Carson Ranger District) USDAFS.
Difficulty: Easy.
Length: 1.6 mile loop.
Elevation: 7,100 feet.
Special attractions: Spooner Lake.
Water: None.
Best season: Summer through fall.
For more information: Nevada Division of State Parks, 1060 Mallory Way, Carson City, NV 89701; (702) 885-4379.
Permit: None.

Finding the trailhead: From Carson City drive south on U.S. Highway 395 three miles then turn west on U.S. Highway 50.
Continue ten miles then turn north on Nevada Highway 28 and park.

The hike: The trail is an easy loop around the shore of Spooner Lake. The Spooner Lake area was a transitory camp for the Washoe Indians and their predecessors as long as 7,000 years ago. As they migrated from the Carson and Eagle Valleys to Lake Tahoe each summer, these people would use the Spooner area as a rest camp.

Starting in the 1870s, Spooner became a collection point for wood being transported from Glenbrook Bay to the Comstock Mines at Virginia City. A small dam built in the 1850s created a mill pond for use by the loggers. The present dam was built in about 1929 for irrigation.—*Nevada Division of Parks*

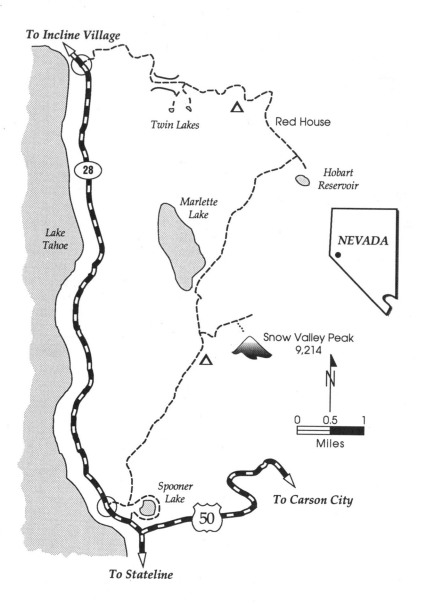

To Incline Village

Twin Lakes

Red House

△

28

Hobart
Reservoir

*Marlette
Lake*

*Lake
Tahoe*

NEVADA

△

Snow Valley Peak
9,214

N

0   0.5   1
Miles

*Spooner
Lake*

50

To Carson City

To Stateline

HIKE 23 *MARLETTE LAKE*

General description: A day hike or overnight backpack trip in the Carson Range.

General location: 13 miles west of Carson City.

Maps: Marlette Lake 7.5-minute, Glenbrook 7.5-minute USGS, Toiyabe National Forest (Carson Ranger District) USDAFS.

Difficulty: Moderate.

Length: 5 miles one way.

Elevation: 7,100 to 8,000 feet.

Special attractions: Marlette Lake.

Water: North Canyon Creek.

Best season: Summer through fall.

For more information: Nevada Division of State Parks, 1060 Mallory Way, Carson City, NV 89701; (702) 885-4379.

Permit: None.

Finding the trailhead: From Carson City, drive south on U.S. Highway 395 three miles, then turn west on U.S. Highway 50. Continue ten miles then turn north on Nevada Highway 28 and park.

The hike: The trail generally follows North Canyon Creek for about five miles to Marlette Lake, a man made reservoir. There is designated camping near the turnoff to Snow Valley Peak, four miles from the trailhead.

Marlette Lake was constructed as the centerpiece of the elaborate water system supplying 25,000 to 40,000 people at Virginia City and Carson City. The chimney standing on the southeastern shore of the lake was once part of the watermaster's house, occupied until the late 1950s. The dam was originally built in 1873 to aid in fluming wood to Spooner Summit and then on to Carson City. It has since undergone several reconstructions and is presently fifty-two feet high. The lake water is still used as a backup supply for Virginia City and Carson City. It is also used by the Nevada Department of Wildlife as a breeding area for cutthroat trout and is closed to fishing.

From near the designated camp site, a side trip can be made about one mile to 9,214-foot Snow Valley Peak. A watershed rehabilitation project developed by the USDA Forest Service is visible on the eastern slope. The area was originally decimated by logging and then by forty years of over grazing by sheep.

It is possible to continue about three miles to the Hobart Reservoir Trail, and then hike another six miles to the Hidden Beach Trailhead.—*Nevada Division of Parks*

HIKE 24 *JONES CREEK—WHITES CREEK TRAIL*

General description: A day hike in the Carson Range.
General location: About 10 miles southwest of Reno.
Maps: Mount Rose 7.5-minute, Mount Rose NW 7.5-minute, Mount Rose NE 7.5-minute, Washoe City 7.5-minute USGS, Toiyabe National Forest (Carson Ranger District) USDAFS.
Difficulty: Difficult.
Length: 8-mile loop.
Elevation: 6,200 to 8,300 feet.
Special attractions: Outstanding views.
Water: Jones and Whites Creek are permanent streams.
Best season: Summer through fall.
For more information: Toiyabe National Forest, Carson Ranger District, 1536 S. Carson St., Carson City, NV 89701; (702) 882-2766.
Permit: None.

Finding the trailhead: From Reno drive eight miles south on U.S. Highway 395 then turn right (west) on Nevada Highway 431. Continue four miles west to Galena Creek Park. The trailhead is located at the north picnic area.

The hike: The trail follows a jeep road for about 0.5 mile and then crosses Jones Creek. At the trail junction turn right (east) to start the loop trail, which heads in a northerly direction. Climbing gradually through stands of Jeffrey pine and mountain mahogany, the trail enters Whites Canyon and then turns sharply west. Continue on the old road approximately 1.5 miles. After entering the Mount Rose Wilderness, the trail turns right (leaving the old road), crosses Whites Creek and heads west. At about the halfway point, the trail leaves Whites Canyon to the southeast and climbs onto an 8,000 foot ridge with excellent views. About a mile farther on, a spur trail leads west about 0.5 miles to a small lake, locally called Church's Pond. James E. Church was a professor at the University of Nevada Reno who established the first winter snow survey in the world. He devised his system on Mount Rose early in this century. Snow surveys are used to predict the amount of spring runoff that fills the reservoirs that supply water to lowland farms and cities.

The main trail continues east, switchbacking down into Jones Creek to complete the loop. At the trail junction turn right (southeast) and follow the trail 0.5 miles to the trailhead.

Mountain mahogany is found here and is common throughout most of Nevada's mountain ranges. Not related to the tropical mahogany used for cabinet making, mountain mahogany is a fifteen to thirty foot evergreen tree with narrow, shiny, dark green leathery leaves. It may have received its name from the dark reddish-brown mahogany-colored heartwood. Native Americans made a red dye from its roots.—*USDA Forest Service and Bruce Grubbs*

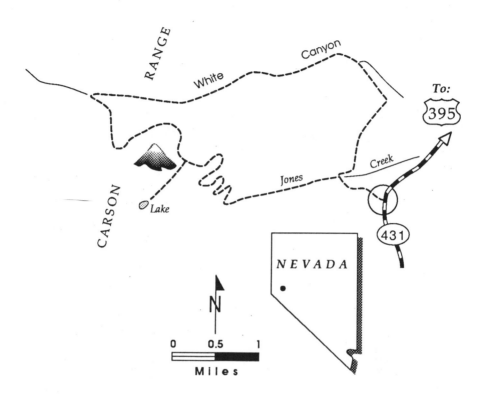

HIKE 25 *MOUNT ROSE*

General description: A day hike in the Carson Range.
General location: About 15 miles southwest of Reno.
Maps: Mount Rose 7.5-minute USGS, Toiyabe National Forest (Carson Ranger District) USDAFS.
Difficulty: Difficult.
Length: 6 miles one way.
Elevation: 8,800 to 10,776 feet.
Special attractions: Spectacular views of the Lake Tahoe region of the Sierra Nevada.
Water: None.
Best season: Summer through fall.
For more information: Toiyabe National Forest, Carson Ranger District, 1536 S. Carson St., Carson City, NV 89701; (702) 882-2766.
Permit: None.

Finding the trailhead: From Reno drive eight miles south on U.S. Highway 395 then turn right (west) on Nevada Highway 431. The trailhead is at the maintenance station just beyond Mount Rose Summit. This is also the upper Ophir Creek trailhead.

The hike: For 2.5 miles the trail climbs gradually on a dirt road. The trail then turns right, leaving the road, and crosses the headwaters basin of Galena Creek. After crossing the creek, the trail heads steeply uphill. At the halfway point, the trail crosses a saddle, entering the Mount Rose Wilderness, and again turns to the right heading north toward Mount Rose. The last two miles are steep and difficult. The 360-degree view from the summit includes Lake Tahoe, the Great Basin Ranges to the east, and Reno to the north. Hikers should beware of the strong winds that rake the mountain above timberline on most afternoons.

The beautiful and famous Lake Tahoe is one of the highest large lakes in the world, but it is only a small remnant of the great Lake Lahontan system, which covered many of the valleys in northwestern Nevada during the last glacial period. Looking at the dry desert valleys with their alkaline sinks and scanty vegetation, it is hard to believe that the view eastward was as green and forested 10,000 years ago as the view to the west is now.—*USDA Forest Service and Bruce Grubbs*

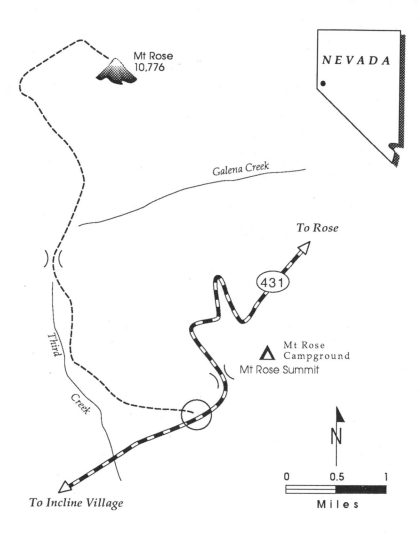

Mt Rose
10,776

NEVADA

Galena Creek

To Rose

431

Mt Rose
Campground

Mt Rose Summit

Third

Creek

N

To Incline Village

0   0.5   1

Miles

HIKE 26 OPHIR CREEK TRAIL

General description: A day hike in the Carson Range near Lake Tahoe.
General location: 2 miles southwest of Washoe City.
Maps: Washoe City 7.5-minute, Mount Rose 7.5-minute USGS, Toiyabe National Forest (Carson Ranger District) USDAFS.
Difficulty: Difficult.
Length: 6 miles one way.
Elevation: 5,300 to 8,600 feet.
Special attractions: Opportunity to view the results of a massive land slide.
Water: None.
Best season: Spring through fall.
For more information: Toiyabe National Forest, Carson Ranger District, 1536 S. Carson St., Carson City, NV 89701; (702) 882-2766.
Permit: None.

Finding the trailhead: To reach the lower (eastern) trailhead from Reno drive south on U.S. Highway 395 and turn right one mile south of Washoe City. After 0.5 miles turn right to Davis Creek County Park.

The hike: This hike is a difficult and strenuous climb up the Ophir Creek drainage to the remains of Upper and Lower Price Lakes, which were destroyed when part of Slide Mountain fell into them in 1983. The resulting mud and water accumulation rushed down the Ophir Creek drainage and created a massive movement of earth that was deposited at Washoe Lake. It also removed part of the trail. Three miles from the western end, the trail turns into a jeep road that is open to hiking only. The last three miles also parallel scenic Tahoe Meadows; the trail ends at Nevada Highway 431. There is a new trailhead 0.5 mile to the east along the highway. This trailhead is shared with the Mount Rose Trail.

The tall pines featuring three long needles per bundle commonly found in the Carson Range and the Sierra Nevada are Jeffrey pine. These beautiful trees closely resemble the ponderosa pine found in eastern and southern Nevada ranges, but are distinguished by the lighter color of their needles and by the unique strong smell of vanilla or lemon given off by crushed needles or twigs.—*USDA Forest Service and Bruce Grubbs*

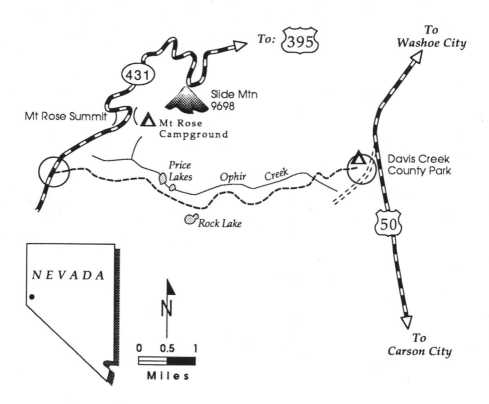

HIKE 27 GRIMES POINT ARCHAEOLOGICAL AREA

General description: A day hike on an interpretive trail.
General location: 10 miles east of Fallon.
Maps: Grimes Point 7.5-minute USGS.
Difficulty: Easy.
Length: About 1 mile.
Elevation: 4,000 to 4,200 feet.
Special attractions: Petroglyphs, pictographs, rock shelters and caves.
Water: None.
Best season: September through May.
For more information: Bureau of Land Management, Carson City District Office, 1535 Hot Springs Rd., #300, Carson City, NV 89701; (702) 882-1631.
Permit: None.

Finding the trailhead: The Grimes Point Archaeological Site is located on U.S. Highway 50 about ten miles east of Fallon. The Petroglyph Trail is located near the highway. The Hidden Cave Trail begins 1.5 miles north of the Grimes Point turnoff from US 50, and access is via a well-maintained gravel road.

The hike: The Grimes Point Archaeological Area contains two interpretive trails. The easy Petroglyph Trail is a short trail through a petroglyph boulder field. The longer Hidden Cave Trail provides access to petroglyphs, rock shelters, and geological features. Hidden Cave is a major archaeological site used prehistorically by hunter-gatherers as a cache or storage site. The cave was occupied between 3,400 to 4,000 years ago.

Free public tours of the cave begin in Fallon at 10 a.m. on the second and fourth Saturday each month. The trails are open to the public all year.

From the Grimes Point area, it is possible to see a series of horizontal lines on the distant mountains. These are wave terraces cut into the slopes by the waters of ancient Lake Lahontan, which reached depths of seven hundred feet. Although Grimes Point is a dry, desolate area at present, 10,000 years ago it was a rich lakeshore, teeming with life. Given those conditions, it is not surprising that the ancient people spent a lot of time here.—*Bureau of Land Management and Bruce Grubbs*

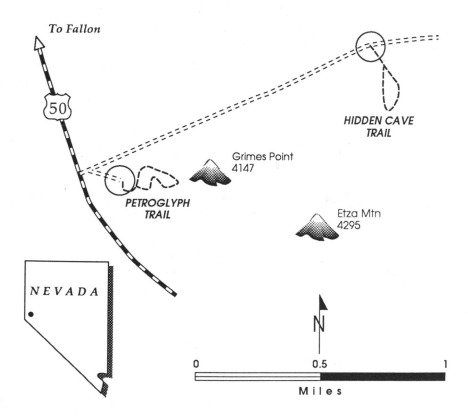

To Fallon

50

HIDDEN CAVE
TRAIL

Grimes Point
4147

PETROGLYPH
TRAIL

Etza Mtn
4295

NEVADA

N

0   0.5   1

Miles

HIKE 28 *SAND SPRINGS DESERT STUDY AREA*

General description: Interpretive day hike through sand dune area.
General location: 25 miles southeast of Fallon.
Maps: Fourmile Flat 7.5-minute USGS.
Difficulty: Easy.
Length: 0.5-mile loop.
Elevation: 4,000 feet.
Special attractions: Pony Express station, sand dunes.
Water: None.
Best Season: September through May.
For more information: Bureau of Land Management, Carson City District Office, 1535 Hot Springs Rd., #300, Carson City, NV 89701; (702) 882-1631.
Permit: None.

Finding the trailhead: From Fallon drive east about twenty-three miles on U.S. Highway 50 to the Sand Springs Desert Study Area.

The hike: The Sand Springs Desert Study Area is located in a fifty-acre area closed to off-road vehicles just south of Sand Mountain. Sand Mountain is approximately 3.5 miles long, one mile wide, and rises about 600 feet above the valley floor making it the largest single dune in the Great Basin. The interpretive trail is accessible by dirt road approximately 1.5 miles north of US 50. The hiker can learn about the unique sand dune environment and view a Pony Express station along with other historic features.

Although many people unfamiliar with it think of the American desert as a vast area of sand dunes, the Sand Springs area is typical of sand dune areas in the Southwest. A particular combination of circumstances must combine before dunes are formed. There must be a supply of sand, prevailing winds tending to push the sand in the same direction, and a topographic feature acting as a trap to contain the sand. Here the surrounding mountains capture the wind blown grains.

It can be especially rewarding to explore the dunes at sunrise. The slanting sunlight emphasizes the texture of the surface and clearly shows the tracks and activities of animals active on the sand during the cool night hours.—
Bureau of Land Management and Bruce Grubbs

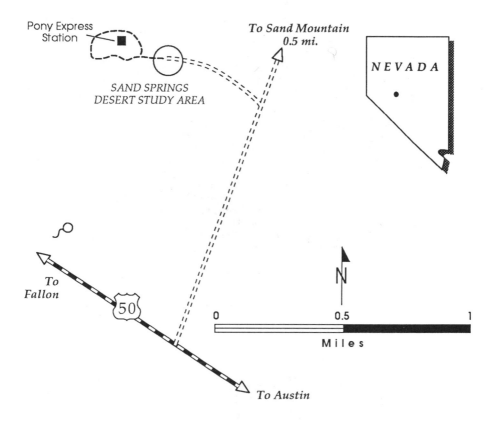

CENTRAL NEVADA

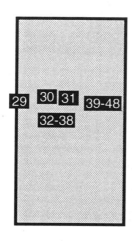

29. Cold Springs Pony Express Station
30. Berlin—Ichthyosaur State Park
31. Toiyabe Crest Trail
32. Stewart Creek Trail
33. North Twin River Trail
34. South Twin River Trail
35. Jett Canyon Trail
36. Toms Canyon
37. Peavine Canyon
38. Cow Canyon Trail
39. Pine Creek Trail
40. Pasco Canyon Trail
41. Mount Jefferson Crest Trail
42. Morgan Creek to Cottonwood Creek
43. Mosquito Creek Trail
44. North Mosquito Creek Trail
45. South Mosquito Creek Trail
46. Barley Creek Trail
47. Green Monster Trail
48. Clear Lake Trail

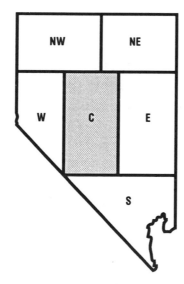

HIKE 29 COLD SPRINGS PONY EXPRESS STATION

General description: A day hike to a Pony Express station.
General location: 51 miles west of Austin.
Maps: Cold Springs 7.5-minute USGS.
Difficulty: Easy.
Length: 1.5 miles one way.
Elevation: 5,480 to 5,800 feet.
Special attractions: Scenic views of Desatoya Mountains, Pony Express Historic Site.
Best season: Late spring through fall.
For more information: Bureau of Land Management, Carson City District Office, 1535 Hot Springs Rd., #300, Carson City, NV 89701; (702) 882-1631.
Permit: None.

Finding the trailhead: From Austin go fifty-one miles east on U.S. Highway 50 to the Pony Express interpretive sign.

The hike: The Cold Springs Trail begins near US 50 at an interpretive display that describes the Pony Express. The Pony Express delivered mail by horseback during 1860-1861 from Missouri to California. This hiking trail provides access to a well-preserved Pony Express station. Other historic sites in the vicinity include an overland stage and a transcontinental telegraph station.

The Pony Express only operated for a year and a half but became famous for the speed and dangers of its service. Mail, at the rate of five dollars per half ounce, was carried nearly two thousand miles from St. Joseph to San Francisco in ten days by riders covering sixty to one hundred miles at a full gallop. Stations were twenty-five miles apart, and the riders stopped only to change horses. Several station men and at least one rider were lost to hostile Indian attacks. Advertisements for riders requested young men without family ties, preferably orphans, who were willing to risk death daily. Late in 1861, the first successful telegraph message was sent between the same cities, ending the need for the Pony Express.—*Bureau of Land Management and Bruce Grubbs*

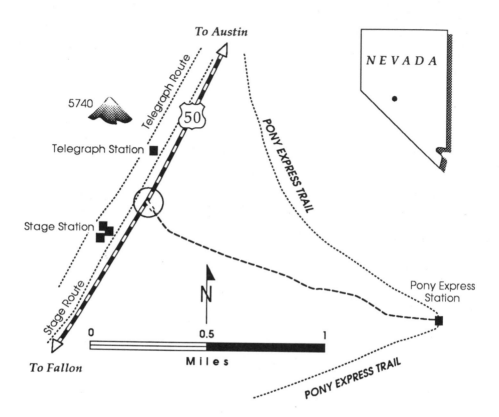

HIKE 30 BERLIN-ICHTHYOSAUR STATE PARK

General description: A day hike in an old mining town.
General location: 23 miles northwest of Gabbs.
Maps: Ione 7.5-minute, Grantsville 7.5-minute USGS, Toiyabe National Forest (Tonopah Ranger District) USDAFS.
Difficulty: Easy.
Length: Approximately a 1-mile loop.
Elevation: 7,000.
Special attractions: Turn of the century mining town.
Water: At ranger station and campground.
Best season: Late spring through fall.
For more information: Nevada Division of State Parks, 1060 Mallory Way, Carson City, NV 89701; (702) 885-4379.
Permit: None.

Finding the trailhead: From Gabbs drive north on Nevada Highway 361 about three miles then turn east on Nevada Highway 844. Continue approximately twenty miles on this maintained dirt road to Berlin-Ichthyosaur State Park.

The hike: A self-guided trail leads through the old town of Berlin, with extensive signs explaining the history and features. A nature trail also leads from the campground to the Ichthyosaur fossil shelter.

The mining history of the area started in 1863 when a group of prospectors discovered silver in Union Canyon. The Union Mining District was formed in 1864, but the Berlin Mine wasn't established until 1895. The town of Berlin was now in its heyday, which lasted until 1911. At its peak Berlin and its suburbs included about 250 people. Many buildings from this period still remain. The Berlin Mine, a shaft mine with three miles of tunnels, produced approximately $849,000 of gold.

Ichthyosaurs, meaning "fish-lizards," were a group of highly specialized marine reptiles. Fossils of these animals have been found dating back to 240 million years ago, and the ichthyosaurs became extinct ninety million years ago. During this time they seem to have occupied the same ecological niche as toothed whales and dolphins. Ichthyosaurs ranged in length from two to fifty feet.

The oldest rocks in the park area are volcanic deposits of unknown age. But the rocks exposed in Union Canyon are marine limestones resulting from an inland sea from the Mesozoic Era (245 to 65 million years ago). The ichthyosaurs lived in this sea and when they died; the carcasses sank to the seafloor where they were slowly covered with hundreds of feet of sediments. Later, as great continental blocks of the earth's crust collided to expand the North American Continent westward, the sea floor rose and the ocean drained. About 34 million years ago, the region was buried in lava flows and ash falls from massive volcanism. Only in recent time, geologically speaking, has faulting and uplifting created the basin and range topography characterizing the region today. During this process most of the volcanic rock was eroded away, exposing the marine sediments of Union Canyon.—*Nevada Division of State Parks*

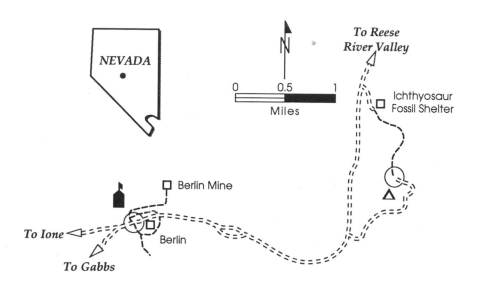

The Toiyabe Crest Trail traverses the spectacular south half of the Toiyabe Range, making it one of the longest trails in Nevada.

HIKE 31 *TOIYABE CREST TRAIL*

General description: A six- to seven-day backpack in the Toiyabe Range.
General location: 35 miles south of Austin.
Maps: Brewer Canyon 7.5-minute, Millet Ranch 7.5-minute, Tierney Creek 7.5-minute, South Toiyabe Peak 7.5-minute, Carvers NW 7.5-minute, Arc Dome 7.5-minute, Bakeoven Creek 7.5-minute USGS, Toiyabe National Forest (Austin Ranger District), Toiyabe National Forest (Tonopah Ranger District) USDAFS.
Difficulty: Difficult.
Length: Approximately 67 miles one way.
Elevation: 6,345 to 11,775 feet.
Special attractions: The Toiyabe Crest National Recreation Trail, featuring far-ranging alpine and desert views, aspens, and alpine streams.
Water: Numerous creeks and springs.
Best season: Summer through fall.
For more information: Toiyabe National Forest, Austin Ranger District, Austin, NV 89310; (702) 964-2671; Toiyabe National Forest, Tonopah Ranger District, P.O. Box 3940, Tonopah, NV 89049-3940; (702) 482-6286.
Permit: None.

Finding the trailhead: From Austin, drive east on U.S. Highway 50, then south on Nevada Highway 376. Approximately twenty-seven miles from Austin, turn west on the dirt Kingston Creek road. Park eight miles from the highway at the head of a reservoir, opposite an abandoned ranch. There is no trailhead sign, but the Crest Trail is obvious; it switchbacks up the slope to the south.

The trip will require a car be left at the southern trailhead, South Twin River. See Hike 34 for trailhead access information from South Twin River.

The hike: Although depicted fairly accurately on the topographic maps, the trail is old and receives little maintenance. Sections of old trail confuse the route, and new roads have been constructed in some of the side canyons. The hiker should have the topographic maps and some experience in off trail route finding.

During early summer, water is plentiful as most drainages and springs will be flowing. Also, there will be snow to melt along the higher sections. Late in the summer and into fall, it may be necessary to carry more water along the drier sections, especially at the north end of the trip.

From 7,500 feet elevation at the trailhead, the trail climbs steeply to the crest over a distance of several miles, and reaches a flat-topped section of ridge at 10,400 feet. The trail stays along the crest until it descends into an aspen grove at the head of Washington Creek, where there is good camping.

South of Washington Creek, the trail traverses the northwest slopes of Toiyabe Range Peak. The 10,960-foot peak is an easy climb, and the views of the desert 6,000 feet below and the adjoining ranges are well worth the effort. Boundary Peak in the White Mountains, the highest point in Nevada, is visible far to the southwest.

Continuing on the trail, there is good camping in an aspen grove on the west ridge of Toiyabe Range Peak. To the south, the trail stays on the west side of the crest as it heads the numerous forks of San Juan and Tierney Creeks.

HIKE 31 *TOIYABE CREST TRAIL—NORTH HALF*

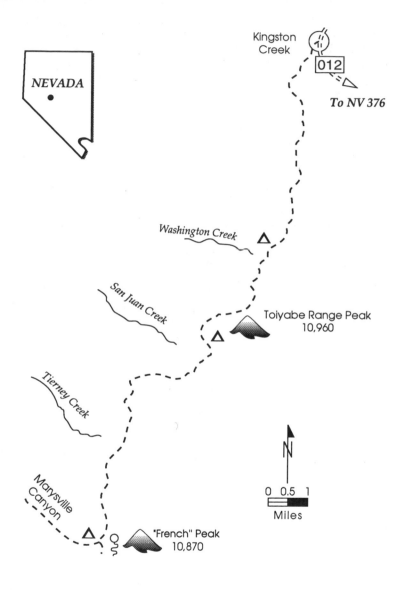

This is the faintest section of the trail, and it may be lost occasionally. The spring at the head of Marysville Canyon provides good camping.

The trail south of "French" Peak (10,780 feet) is more evident. After crossing Ophir Summit and the end of Forest Road 017, the trail continues south toward Arc Dome. About two miles south of Ophir Summit, it is possible to end the trip early by turning east on the North Twin River Trail and descending about

Lack of summer rain and a long, cold winter make life difficult for trees in the Toiyabe Range.

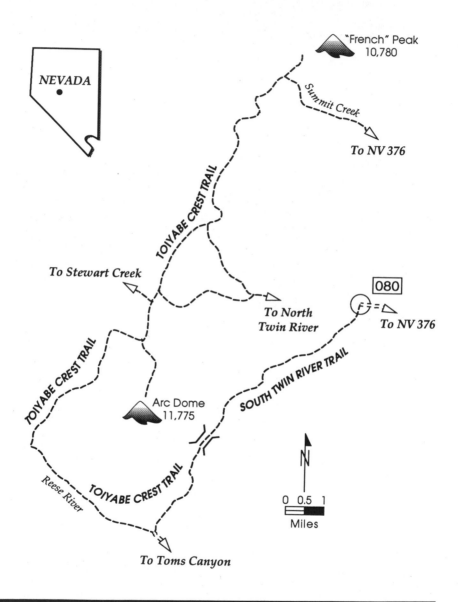

seven miles to the trailhead. See Hike 33 North Twin River Trail description for details.

The Crest Trail continues along the main crest. In three miles, another trail descends east to the North Twin River Trail. About 0.5 mile farther south, the Crest Trail meets the Stewart Creek Trail, which descends to the northwest. Finally, the Crest Trail itself leaves the crest to the west, about 1.5 miles south of the junction with the Stewart Creek Trail, and descends west into Sawmill Creek.

Before leaving the crest, a worthwhile side trip can be made to the 11,775-foot summit of Arc Dome. This hike is about two miles one way.

The Crest Trail then follows Sawmill Creek south for about five miles to the Reese River, where it turns southeast up the river. In just over a mile, the Peavine Canyon Trail comes in from the south. About four miles farther, the Reese River turns sharply to the northeast, and the Toms Canyon trail joins by way of Trail Canyon. The Crest Trail continues four miles to a pass at the head of the Reese River, where it meets the South Twin River Trail. See Hike 34 South Twin River Trail description for the remainder of the hike.

The Toiyabe Crest Trail and its spur trails were constructed by the Civilian Conservation Corps during the 1930s. Evidence of their skilled work still survives today along the trails. Although the Toiyabe Range is well watered for a Nevada mountain range, it has noticeably less trees than the ranges farther to the east. This is probably due to the lack of summer rain. In the Southwest, most summer rain comes in the form of afternoon thunderstorms, which form in warm humid air moving up from the Gulf of Mexico. Central Nevada is too far from the source of moisture to have reliable summer rains.

HIKE 32 *STEWART CREEK TRAIL*

General description: A long day hike or overnight backpack trip in the Arc Dome Wilderness.

General location: Approximately 80 miles northwest of Tonopah.

Maps: Corral Wash 7.5-minute, Bakeoven Creek 7.5-minute, South Toiyabe Peak 7.5-minute, Arc Dome 7.5-minute USGS, Toiyabe National Forest (Tonopah Ranger District) USDAFS.

Difficulty: Moderate.

Length: 5 miles one way.

Elevation: Approximately 9,500 to 11,773 feet.

Special attractions: Access to Arc Dome and the Crest Trail.

Water: Seasonal springs.

Best season: Summer through fall.

For more information: Toiyabe National Forest, Tonopah Ranger District, P.O. Box 3940, Tonopah, NV 89049-3940; (702) 482-6286.

Permit: None.

Finding the trailhead: From Tonopah drive west about six miles on U.S. Highway 95 to the Gabbs Poleline Road. Continue on the Poleline Road then turn east on the Cloverdale road. Just past the old Cloverdale Ranch turn east on Forest Road 018. Continue thirty miles to the Reese River administrative site, then turn east on Forest Road 119; follow this road thirteen miles to its end at Columbine Campground.

The hike: The trail starts at Columbine Campground and goes up an unnamed fork of Stewart Creek. It is a steady climb that becomes steeper near the head of the canyon where it switchbacks up to meet the Toiyabe Crest National Recreation Trail to the west of the main ridge. Turn right (south) onto the Crest Trail, and follow the Crest Trail as it climbs through a 10,600 foot saddle. Just beyond this saddle, a side trail descends east into the North Twin River drainage. The Crest Trail climbs a short drainage to the south, then goes about 1.5 miles along a broad, 11,200 foot ridge. It then drops into an 10,700-foot saddle before starting the steep 1,000-foot climb to the summit of Arc Dome.— *USDA Forest Service and Bruce Grubbs*

HIKE 32 *STEWART CREEK TRAIL*

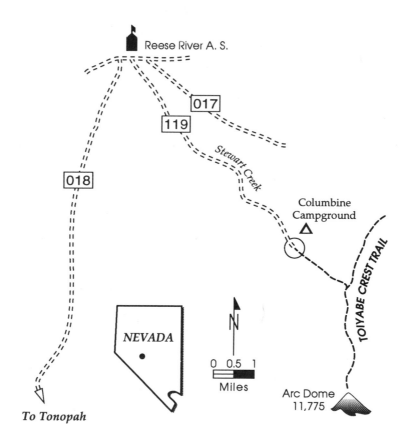

HIKE 33 NORTH TWIN RIVER TRAIL

General description: A long day hike or two- to three-day backpack trip into the Arc Dome Wilderness.

General location: 73 miles north of Tonopah.

Maps: Carvers NW 7.5-minute, South Toiyabe Peak 7.5-minute, Arc Dome 7.5-minute USGS, Toiyabe National Forest (Tonopah Ranger District) USDAFS.

Difficulty: Difficult.

Length: 8 miles one way.

Elevation: 6,400 to 9,300 feet.

Special attractions: Access to a spectacular canyon, and the Toiyabe Crest Trail.

Water: Seasonal springs.

Best season: Summer through fall.

For more information: Toiyabe National Forest, Tonopah Ranger District, P.O. Box 3940, Tonopah, NV 89049-3940; (702) 482-6286.

Permit: None.

Finding the trailhead: From Tonopah drive six miles east on U.S. Highway 95 then turn north on Nevada Highway 376. At the signed North Twin River road (Forest Road 080, about sixty-seven miles from Tonopah) turn west and continue six miles to the trail head.

The hike: This is a loop hike, using the South Twin River and North Twin River trails. Although it can be done in one long day, there are plenty of side attractions that make this a possible two- or three-day backpack trip.

Although many ranges in Nevada don't have forests one would expect from the elevation and climate, quaking aspens grow in nearly every range.

The North Twin River tumbles through an aspen grove in the Toiyabe Range.

To start, walk one mile down the access road to the South Twin River trailhead. Hike up the obvious but unsigned trail that climbs the slope east of the canyon. One large switchback takes you to a saddle overlooking the spectacular lower South Twin River canyon, a gorge rivaling the Granite Gorge of the Grand Canyon. The trail contours to another pass, and an old jeep road joins from the right. This road was built to allow motorized access to a mine within the wilderness area, and is open only to the permittee. Fortunately, the miner doesn't seem to be using it.

After the second saddle, the trail drops into the creek. It stays along the creek, crossing as necessary. The canyon walls tower high above, and there are places where it seems unlikely that a trail would have been built. About three miles from the trailhead, you'll see the ruins of an old water wheel and ore crusher on the left. Although much of the structure has collapsed, the water wheel can still be turned by hand. Just beyond the ruin, there is a fine campsite. Within a short distance, the mine road turns left up the south fork. The South Twin River trail, signed the Crest Trail, continues up the main fork and becomes a foot trail.

After a steep climb through another deep, narrow canyon, the trail levels out somewhat as the canyon opens out, providing views of the high country. In 1.5 miles, turn right (west) at the trail going up the north fork of the South Twin River, which is signed for the North Twin River. There is limited camping at this junction. (Another side trail climbs to the summit of Arc Dome about two miles farther along the South Twin River Trail. A mile after this junction, the trail reaches a pass at the head of the Reese River and joins the Toiyabe Crest National Recreation Trail.

The main trail up the north fork climbs steadily along the right side of the canyon. Water is available intermittently, but other sections of the creek are dry. The trail is distinct and easy to follow, but watch for an abrupt switchback near the head of the canyon, about two miles from the junction. The switchback leads through a dense stand of mountain mahogany to the pass between the South and North Twin Rivers.

Dropping off the saddle to the north, the trail passes the springs shown on the topographic map, and appear to be reliable. The trail stays generally west of the creek for the first mile then descends to the creek through a stand of aspen. About 0.7 miles beyond this point, a side canyon comes in from the west, and there is a signed trail turning left here that goes to the Crest Trail. Only the first 0.2 miles of this side trail is shown on the topographic map.

Continue down the North Twin River Trail through more magnificent aspens. In 0.6 miles there is a second signed trail going left (west) to the Crest Trail, and it is not shown at all on the topographic map. To the right (east) of this junction is a large campsite in the aspen forest.

The main trail stays left of the creek for nearly a mile. Just before it descends to the creek again, it climbs slightly for a nice view of the rugged lower gorge. The last two miles of the trail drop rapidly through the gorge, and the stream noisily follows suit. The aspens give way to narrowleaf cottonwoods, water birch and other lower-elevation growth along the stream. About 0.5 miles from the mouth of the canyon, there is a brief view of the Smoky Valley. Shortly thereafter the trail turns into a jeep road and emerges from the canyon at the trailhead.—*USDA Forest Service and Bruce Grubbs*

The late afternoon sun highlights the rough slopes of the lower North Twin River canyon in the Toiyabe Range. At lower elevations, pinyon pine and juniper trees take over from the bristlecone pines.

HIKE 34 SOUTH TWIN RIVER TRAIL

General description: A day hike in the Toiyabe Range.
General location: 70 miles north of Tonopah.
Maps: Carvers NW 7.5-minute, Arc Dome 7.5-minute USGS, Toiyabe National Forest (Tonopah Ranger District) USDAFS.
Difficulty: Easy.
Length: 0.5 mile one way.
Elevation: 6,200 to 9,240 feet.
Special attractions: Easy walk to a spectacular view of a canyon.
Water: South Twin River at trailhead.
Best season: Spring through fall.
For more information: Toiyabe National Forest, Tonopah Ranger District, P.O. Box 3940, Tonopah, NV 89049-3940; (702) 482-6286.
Permit: None.

HIKES 33 & 34

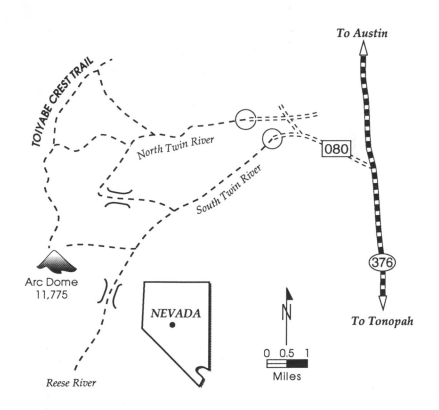

The South Twin River Trail in the Toiyabe Range makes a dramatic entry into the craggy lower canyon. This popular trail connects to the Toiyabe Crest National Scenic Trail, which traverses the entire length of the southern Toiyabe Range.

Old water wheel and rock crusher along the South Twin River in the Toiyabe Range. Most of the machinery is in ruins, but this water wheel still turns freely. Ruins of failed mining ventures are scattered throughout Nevada.

Finding the trailhead: From Tonopah, drive six miles east on U.S. Highway 95 then turn north on Nevada Highway 376 for 60.5 miles. At the signed South Twin River road (Forest Road 080), turn west and continue three miles to the trailhead.

The hike: This is an easy hike with a short, graded access road in a mountain range where most of the hikes are difficult and the access roads long. Hikers can do this hike in an hour or so and get an idea what treats await deeper in the mountains.

The South Twin River Trail is part of the Toiyabe Crest National Recreation Trail, and is visible from the trailhead as it climbs the mountainside in a large switchback. (Ignore the road going into the creek.) This hike takes you up a switchback to the first saddle. From this vantage point, five hundred feet above the trailhead, there is a fine view of the lower South Twin River canyon, with its cascading mountain stream, cottonwood trees, and towering rock walls. In contrast, the vast Smokey Valley spreads out to the north, and the buttresses forming the east slopes of the Toiyabe Range march off into the distance.

For more information on the South Twin River trail, see Hike 33 North Twin River Loop.

HIKE 35 *JETT CANYON TRAIL*

General description: A day hike in the Toiyabe Range.
General location: 60 miles north of Tonopah.
Maps: Pablo Canyon Ranch 7.5-minute, Toms Canyon 7.5-minute, Arc Dome 7.5-minute USGS, Toiyabe National Forest (Tonopah Ranger District) USDAFS.
Difficulty: Easy.
Length: 2 miles one way.
Elevation: 7,400 to 8,700 feet.
Special attractions: Dramatic canyon, bighorn sheep area.
Water: Jett Creek.
Best season: Summer through fall.
For more information: Toiyabe National Forest, Tonopah Ranger District, P.O. Box 3940, Tonopah, NV 89049-3940; (702) 482-6286.
Permit: None.

Finding the trailhead: From Tonopah drive six miles east on U.S. Highway 95 then turn north on Nevada Highway 376 for 47.7 miles. At the signed Jett Canyon road (Forest Road 090), turn west and continue five miles to a cattleguard at the mouth of the canyon and park on the right. The road turns into a jeep road here and is normally closed with a locked gate about 0.3 mile farther.

The hike: This is an easy walk up a deep, narrow canyon. The rugged walls are ideal bighorn sheep country, and the alert hiker may see a band running casually across impossible-looking terrain. The trail continues about five miles up the canyon before ending near the head of the drainage, but stopping after two miles keeps this an easy hike, if desired. It is possible for those skilled

The steep, rocky slopes of Jett Canyon in the southern Toiyabe Range are prime habitat for bighorn sheep. The animals are never seen very far from steep cliffs and rocky slopes, which they traverse with light-footed ease.

in cross-country hiking and map reading to continue beyond the end of the trail into the Arc Dome Wilderness area.—*USDA Forest Service and Bruce Grubbs*

HIKE 35 *JETT CANYON TRAIL*

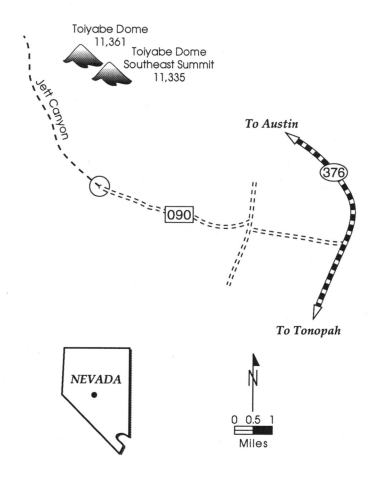

Toiyabe Dome
11,361
Toiyabe Dome
Southeast Summit
11,335

Jett Canyon

To Austin

376

090

To Tonopah

NEVADA

N

0 0.5 1

Miles

HIKE 36 *TOMS CANYON*

General description: An overnight or longer backpack trip in the Toiyabe Range.

General location: 50 miles north of Tonopah.

Maps: Toms Canyon 7.5-minute, Arc Dome 7.5-minute USGS, Toiyabe National Forest (Tonopah Ranger District) USDAFS.

Difficulty: Moderate.

Length: 10 miles one way.

Elevation: 7,360 to 9,360 feet.

Special attractions: Access to the upper Reese River country and Peavine and Mahogany Mountains.

Water: At trailhead and seasonal springs.

Best season: Summer through fall.

For more information: Toiyabe National Forest, Tonopah Ranger District, P.O. Box 3940, Tonopah, NV 89049-3940; (702) 482-6286.

Permit: None.

Finding the trailhead: From Tonopah drive east on U.S. Highway 95 for six miles then turn north on Nevada Highway 376. Continue 34.5 miles to the Peavine Campground turnoff (Forest Road 020). Follow this gravel road past the campground to a signed junction at 14.5 miles. Turn right and drive 0.7 mile to the trailhead. There is good camping and also water in the creek at the trailhead.

The hike: The Toms Canyon Trail follows the canyon for about 0.3 mile then exits the canyon via an unnamed drainage to the north. About three miles from the trailhead, the trail crosses a 9,360-foot pass between Peavine and the Mahogany Mountains. This pass is a good destinatin for a day hike. The trail continues north down Trail Creek about two miles to join the Toiyabe Crest National Recreation Trail. A three-day loop trip could be done using the Peavine Canyon Trail, and longer trips could use the Crest Trail and the North Twin River Trail.—*USDA Forest Service and Bruce Grubbs*

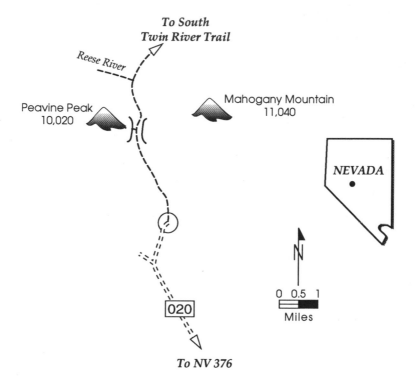

HIKE 37 *PEAVINE CANYON*

General description: A long day hike or overnight backpack trip in the Toiyabe Range.

General location: 50 miles north of Tonopah.

Maps: Toms Canyon 7.5-minute, Farrington Canyon 7.5-minute, Bakeoven Creek 7.5-minute USGS, Toiyabe National Forest (Tonopah Ranger District) USDAFS.

Difficulty: Moderate.

Length: 9 miles one way.

Elevation: 7,200 to 8,634 feet.

Special attractions: Access to the Arc Dome Wilderness from the south.

Water: Peavine Canyon, seasonal springs.

Best season: Summer through fall.

For more information: Toiyabe National Forest, Tonopah Ranger District, P.O. Box 3940, Tonopah, NV 89049-3940; (702) 482-6286.

Permit: None.

Finding the trailhead: From Tonopah drive east on U.S. Highway 95 six miles then turn north on Nevada Highway 376. Continue 47.7 miles to the Peavine Campground turnoff on the left (Forest Road 020). Follow this gravel road past the campground to a signed junction at 14.5 miles. Turn left and continue until the road gets too rough for your vehicle. A high clearance vehicle will be needed to drive to the unsigned trailhead, about 1.9 miles. The road past the

Pinyon pines and junipers dot the sage-covered slopes of Peavine Canyon in the Toiyabe Range, while the valley bottom supports a permanent stream and dense stands of willows.

HIKE 37 *PEAVINE CANYON*

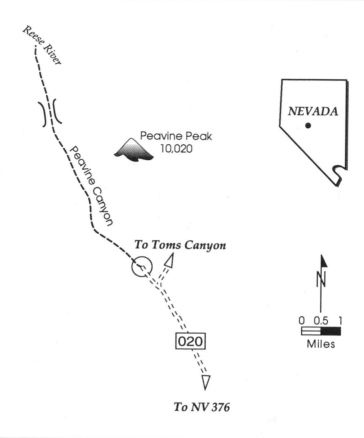

junction is a pleasant walk, and it would be more logical to close the road just past the junction. There are no campsites at the trailhead and there is limited parking.

The hike: The Peavine Canyon Trail follows an old jeep trail initially. It has a much gentler gradient than most Toiyabe trails. The trail stays in Peavine Canyon to its head, crosses a pass at 8,634 feet, then gradually descends a drainage to meet the Toiyabe Crest National Recreation Trail at Reese River. This trail is useful for access to the Crest Trail and could also be used for a three-day backpack in a loop with the Toms Canyon Trail, with a short car shuttle or road walk between trailheads. For an overnight backpack trip, the Reese River is a logical destination.—*USDA Forest Service and Bruce Grubbs*

HIKE 38 *COW CANYON TRAIL*

General description: A day hike in the Toiyabe Range.

General location: About 50 miles northwest of Tonopah.

Maps: Bakeoven Creek 7.5-minute USGS, Toiyabe National Forest (Tonopah Ranger District) USDAFS.

Difficulty: Easy.

Length: 1 mile one way.

Elevation: 7,440 to 8,000 feet.

Special attractions: Easy access to Arc Dome Wilderness and the Toiyabe Crest National Recreation Trail.

Water: None.

Best season: Summer through fall.

For more information: Toiyabe National Forest, Tonopah Ranger District, P.O. Box 3940, Tonopah, NV 89049-3940; (702) 482-6286.

Permit: None.

Finding the trailhead: From Tonopah drive about six miles west on U.S. Highway 95 to the Gabbs Poleline Road. Continue on the Poleline Road approximately thirty miles then turn east on the Cloverdale road. Pass the old Cloverdale Ranch then turn east on Forest Road 018. Continue just past Cloverdale Summit then turn right on Forest Road 121 and stay on this road to its end.

The hike: The trail starts at an 8,000-foot saddle then drops east one mile into the Reese River canyon. This route is a popular, short access to the Reese River country and also connects with the Toiyabe Crest National Recreation Trail. It is possible to do a four-day or longer loop backpack trip, using the Crest Trail and the North Twin River Trail.—*USDA Forest Service.*

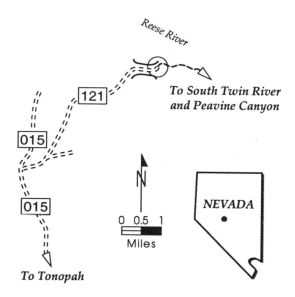

HIKE 39 *PASCO CANYON—PINE CREEK TRAIL*

General description: A two- or three-day backpack in the Toquima Range over Mount Jefferson.
General location: 65 miles northeast of Tonopah.
Maps: Pine Creek Ranch 7.5-minute, Mount Jefferson 7.5-minute USGS, Toiyabe National Forest (Tonopah Ranger District) USDAFS.
Difficulty: Difficult.
Length: 14-mile loop.
Elevation: 7,500 to 11,700 feet.
Special attractions: Access to the Mount Jefferson Plateau.
Water: Pine and Pasco creeks and spring on Mount Jefferson.
Best season: Summer through fall.
For more information: Toiyabe National Forest, Tonopah Ranger District, P.O. Box 3940, Tonopah, NV 89049-3940; (702) 482-6286.
Permit: None.

Finding the trailhead: From Tonopah, drive east about six miles on U.S. Highway 6 then turn north on Nevada Highway 376. After about thirteen miles, turn east (right) on the Monitor Valley road (paved initially but turns to graded dirt after Belmont). Continue on this road 46.5 miles then turn left on the Pine Creek Road (Forest Road 009).

To reach the Pasco Canyon trailhead, which is the start of the hike in this description, go south only 0.4 miles on the Pine Creek Road then turn sharply right (north) onto an unsigned, graded road. After 2.2 miles, turn left (west) at a sign for Pasco Canyon, and continue 2.7 miles to the end of the road. Do not take any of the left turns into the Pasco Canyon Ranch, which is private property.

To reach the Pine Creek Campground trailhead, which is the ending place for this hike, stay on the Pine Creek Road and turn west (right) at a sign for the campground. Then drive another 2.6 miles to the campground. The trailhead is signed and is on the north side of the campground as you enter.

The hike: This description of the loop hike starts at the Pasco Canyon trailhead. With two vehicles, a short car shuttle can be done. Alternatively, the packs could be dropped at the Pasco Canyon trailhead, and a driver could take the vehicle to the Pine Creek trailhead, then do an easy three mile cross country walk along the foothills to reach the Pasco trailhead.

The Monitor Valley road passes through the ghost town of Belmont, a National Historic Site. Belmont got its start in 1866 after silver was discovered in the area. Once a town of more than two thousand residents, Belmont was for a time the county seat. A few people still live there. Belmont has a small mountain stream that runs year-round and two of the most photographed old buildings in the state—the Courthouse and the Cosmopolitan Hotel.

Manhattan, another mining town, is located about fifteen miles west of Belmont and is reached via Forest Road 014. The town started about the same time as Belmont but grew very slowly until 1905, when gold was discovered. By the end of the year more than one thousand people were living in Manhattan. The San Francisco earthquake of 1906 jolted Manhattan indirectly—many

Alpine lake at the head of Pine Creek, Toquima Range. Pine Creek Canyon is the most popular access to the Alta Toquima Wilderness.

A beautiful mixture of mountain-mahogany, quaking aspen, and bristlecone pines cover the upper slopes of Pine Creek in the Toquima Range.

investors withdrew funds from mining stocks and turned to rebuilding San Francisco. The mines in Manhattan virtually ceased production within a month. But rich strikes later that year and the next revived the district, and prospecting and mining has continued to the present time.

Four miles of the hike traverses 11,000-foot Mount Jefferson. The summit plateau is treeless and there is no shelter from high wind or bad weather. Be prepared for windy, cold weather even in summer; if you plan to camp on the summit plateau, make certain you have a good tent.

A sign near the trailhead gives credit to the Tonopah Explorer Scout Post for reconstructing the Pasco Canyon Trail during 1988-1989. The trail contours along the slope to reach the bottom of the canyon. For the next mile, the trail stays in the canyon bottom through a narrow section hemmed in by high cliffs. The trail is overgrown but easy to follow through this section. As the canyon opens out, aspens appear. The trail continues to the last stand of aspens, then fades out. There is a nice view of the North Summit of Mount Jefferson from this open basin, and this is a good destination for an easy day hike.

There is no reliable water source in Pasco Canyon above this point, so those continuing with the loop over the mountain should pick up enough water for the climb ahead. Stay in the canyon bottom another 0.5 mile then start cross country southwest up the ridge just below the word "Pasco" on the topographic map. This ridge leads to the elevation marked 11,188 on the map. The first mile is moderate then the ascent becomes much steeper. After the 11,188 point, follow the ridge top west then southwest over the 11,691-foot summit. Although the map shows a trail here, only faint traces exist. The trails across Mount Jefferson apparently don't get enough use to remain distinct, and there are no cairns. However, it is easy to walk cross country on the open ridges.

Go south through the broad saddle then southwest along the side of the North Summit. West of the North Summit you will come out onto a very flat area at 11,000 feet. A small creek meanders through the alpine tundra and there are plenty of camp sites. The view of the Toiyabe Range to the west is expansive.

Hike southeast to regain the ridge crest then go south, passing the Middle Summit to the east. From here, you can look down at a small lake in the South Fork of Pine Creek and the aspen and pine-filled basin. Continue southeast and head for the upper end of Pine Creek, which is just north of the South Summit. Watch for bighorn sheep in this area. As you drop toward the rim, head for the lowest point. A series of rock cairns mark the beginning of the trail descending into Pine Creek; the trail gets better as you drop over the rim. A sign marks the junction with the south end of the Summit Trail (see Hike 40 Meadow Canyon Trail for more information). Turn left (east) and continue the descent along Pine Creek. After less than a mile, the trail enters a mixed forest of aspen and bristlecone pine, a pleasant sight after the stark summit plateau. In late summer, this section of the creek may be dry. There is reliable water where the trail first crosses to the north side of the creek, and a nice campsite in the aspens. Several avalanche paths funnel major winter snowslides down the north wall of the canyon—the destroyed trees attest to their force.

Just as the trail and the creek enter the lower, craggy section of the canyon (about one mile from the Pine Creek trailhead), there is a cairn marking the trail to Bucks Canyon. Continue down the Pine Creek Trail to the trailhead.

HIKE 40 MEADOW CREEK TRAIL

General description: A day hike in the Toquima Range.
General location: 83 miles north of Tonopah.
Maps: Pine Creek Ranch 7.5-minute, Mount Jefferson 7.5-minute USGS, Toiyabe National Forest (Tonopah Ranger District) USDAFS.
Difficulty: Difficult.
Length: 4 miles one way.
Elevation: 8,200 to 11,700 feet.
Special attractions: Access to the scenic Mount Jefferson crest trail and remote alpine basin.
Water: None.
Best season: Summer through fall.
For more information: Toiyabe National Forest, Tonopah Ranger District, P.O. Box 3940, Tonopah, NV 89049-3940; (702) 482-6286.
Permit: None.

Finding the trailhead: From Tonopah drive east six miles on U.S. Highway 6 then turn north on Nevada Highway 376. After about thirteen miles turn northeast (right) on the Monitor Valley road.

An old stone cabin in Meadow Creek in the Toquima Range is roofed with timber and sod. Stone often was used for building due to the lack of large trees for logs and lumber. In the early mining areas, hundreds of square miles of pinyon juniper forest were clear cut for fuel and mine timbers.

Continue on road past Belmont (where it becomes graded dirt) for 32.3 miles. Then turn left on the signed, and graded Meadow Canyon Road. The road goes through a section of narrow canyon, which eventually opens into a series of meadows. The road passes the Meadow Canyon Guard Station, 8.1 miles from the turnoff; continue on the unmaintained road another 1.2 miles. You will see an unsigned jeep road turning off to the left (north). Park here unless you have a high clearance, four-wheel-drive vehicle.

The hike: Follow the jeep trail as it climbs the ridge just west of the head of Meadow Creek. This section is a steady climb on a moderate grade with panoramic views of the Meadow Creek basin. After about two miles, the jeep trail turns east and contours to Windy Pass, overlooking Andrews Basin. The trail becomes a foot trail after the pass. From here it climbs across the upper section of Andrews Basin and then climbs steeply to the east side of the South Summit of Mountain Jefferson. This point offers sweeping views of Andrew Basin and upper Pine Creek, close at hand, and the Monitor Valley and Monitor Range farther to the east.

The trail descends into the head of Pine Creek to meet the Pine Creek Trail and the Summit Trail. If a car shuttle is used, a traverse of Mount Jefferson can be done, exiting at Pasco Canyon or Moores Creek. See Hike 39 Pasco Canyon-Pine Creek Trail for a traverse of Mount Jefferson with a much shorter car shuttle.—*USDA Forest Service and Bruce Grubbs*

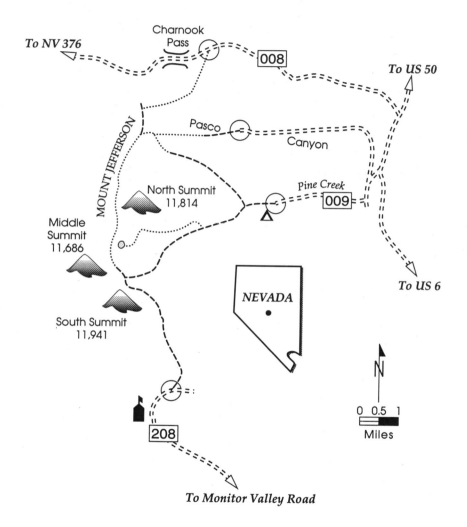

To NV 376

Charnook Pass

008

To US 50

Pasco

Canyon

MOUNT JEFFERSON

North Summit
11,814

Pine Creek

009

Middle
Summit
11,686

To US 6

South Summit
11,941

NEVADA

N

0 0.5 1

Miles

208

To Monitor Valley Road

HIKE 41 *MOORES CREEK TRAIL*

General description: A day hike in the Toquima Range.
General location: 83 miles north of Tonopah.
Maps: Mount Jefferson 7.5-minute, Toiyabe National Forest (Tonopah Ranger District) USDAFS.
Difficulty: Difficult.
Length: 6 miles one way.
Elevation: 7,415 to 11,350 feet.
Special attractions: Access to the north end of the Mount Jefferson Plateau.
Water: Probably in upper Moores Creek.
Best season: Summer through fall.
For more information: Toiyabe National Forest, Tonopah Ranger District, P.O. Box 3940, Tonopah, NV 89049-3940; (702) 482-6286.
Permit: None.

Finding the trailhead: To reach the north trailhead from Tonopah, drive east six miles on U.S. Highway 6 then turn north on Nevada Highway 376 for about sixty-two miles. Turn east on the signed, graded Toquima Range road (Forest Road 008) and go 5.4 miles. Turn right on FR 008. After another 4.9 miles, turn left on the signed Moores Creek FR 008. Continue 7.9 miles to Moores Creek Summit (called Charnock Pass on the maps). Drive east another 0.9 miles, turn right (north) at an old jeep road, and park. This point is 19.1 miles from NV 376.

The hike: The trail follows an old jeep road to a pass at the head of Pasco Canyon. From here contour west cross country into upper Moores Gulch where you will encounter an old trail ascending Moores Creek to the north rim of the Mount Jefferson plateau. At the rim, our destination for this hike, the view is open to the north but somewhat restricted by the points to the east and west. As an option, it is an easy walk cross country about 0.4 mile northwest to point 11,323 for fifty-mile views in three directions.

   This trail could be used for a traverse of Mount Jefferson, by using the Pine Creek or Meadow Creek Trails. See those trail descriptions for more information. Note that travel on Mount Jefferson is essentially cross country; the trails shown on the maps don't get enough use to remain distinct, and they are not marked by blazes or cairns.—*USDA Forest Service and Bruce Grubbs*

HIKE 42 *MORGAN CREEK TRAIL*

General description: A day hike in the Monitor Range.
General location: 70 miles northeast of Tonopah.
Maps: Danville 7.5-minute, Toiyabe National Forest (Tonopah Ranger District) USDAFS.
Difficulty: Difficult.
Length: 2 miles one way.
Elevation: 8,160 to 10,000 feet.
Special attractions: Shortest access to Table Mountain; starting point for crest traverse.
Water: Morgan Creek.
Best season: Summer through fall.
For more information: Toiyabe National Forest, Tonopah Ranger District, P.O. Box 3940, Tonopah, NV 89049-3940; (702) 482-6286.
Permit: None.

Finding the trailhead: From Tonopah, drive east six miles on U.S. Highway 6 then turn north on Nevada Highway 376. After about thirteen miles, turn northeast (right) on the Monitor Valley road.
Continue 45.3 miles on this road, which turns to graded dirt after Belmont. Turn right (northeast) at the signed, graded Morgan Creek-Mosquito Creek road and continue 5.7 miles; then turn left (north) on the Morgan Creek road. Go left at an unsigned fork and then right (east) at the signed turn for Morgan Creek. The trailhead is at the east end of a beautiful stand of aspens, 14.7 miles from the Monitor Valley road. There is good car camping near the trailhead.

The hike: Follow the jeep trail that leaves the parking area to the south. The trail climbs steeply the first mile, then moderates somewhat. The 10,000-foot north end of Table Mountain is reached two miles from the trailhead. This point is the goal for this short but steep hike, where there are good views of the north end of the Monitor Range. This trail can be used to start a traverse of Table Mountain, using the Mosquito Creek, Barley Creek, or Cottonwood Creek Trails as exit points. See those trail descriptions for details.—*USDA Forest Service and Bruce Grubbs*

This small spring in Morgan Creek at the north end of the Monitor Range is a handy water supply. Even when the water flows directly out of a spring, it is still a good idea to purify it chemically, filter it, or boil it before drinking. Even the cleanest looking water may be unsafe.

HIKE 43 MOSQUITO CREEK TRAIL

General description: A long day hike or overnight backpack trip in the Monitor Range.

General location: 70 miles northeast of Tonopah.

Maps: Danville 7.5-minute, Mosquito Creek 7.5-minute USGS, Toiyabe National Forest (Tonopah Ranger District) USDAFS.

Difficulty: Difficult.

Length: 9 miles one way.

Elevation: 7,150 to 10,200 feet.

Special attractions: Access to Table Mountain from the west.

Water: Numerous springs.

Best season: Summer through fall.

For more information: Toiyabe National Forest, Tonopah Ranger District, P.O. Box 3940, Tonopah, NV 89049-3940; (702) 482-6286.

Permit: None.

Finding the trailhead: From Tonopah drive east six miles on U.S. Highway 6 then turn north on Nevada Highway 376. After about thirteen miles turn northeast (right) on the Monitor Valley road.

Continue on this road, which turns to gravel after Belmont, 45.3 miles. Turn right (northeast) at the signed, graded Morgan Creek-Mosquito Creek road and continue 5.7 miles. Then turn right (east) on the Mosquito Creek road (FR 096). Go 2.1 miles to the Mosquito Creek trailhead, which is signed.

Bristlecone pines are rugged, ancient trees that grow near timberline on mountains in Nevada, western Utah, and northern Arizona. Some are more than 6,000 years old. This bristlecone is on the slopes of Mount Jefferson in the Toquima Range.

The hike: The Mosquito Creek trail is not signed but is used regularly (especially by horse parties) and is very easy to follow. Start by going south from the parking area and crossing the creek. Turn left (southeast) at a fork in the trail just after crossing the creek. The trail climbs onto the ridge south of Mosquito Creek and follows it southeast about 3.5 miles. It then crosses a pass at 9,400 feet and then descends and crosses the south fork of Mosquito Creek before making the final climb to Table Mountain.

This trail is much longer than the Morgan Creek Trail, and it climbs more slowly up the gentle western slope of Table Mountain.
An obvious loop could be made with the South Mosquito Creek Trail, but that loop should start with the South Mosquito Trail as it is the harder trail to find. Other possibilities are traverses of Table Mountain, exiting at Barley Creek or Cottonwood Creek.—*USDA Forest Service and Bruce Grubbs*

HIKE 44 *NORTH MOSQUITO CREEK TRAIL*

General description: A day hike in the Monitor Range.
General location: 70 miles northeast of Tonopah.
Maps: Danville 7.5-minute, Mosquito Creek 7.5-minute USGS, Toiyabe National Forest (Tonopah Ranger District) USDAFS.
Difficulty: Difficult.
Length: 5 miles one way.
Elevation: 6,911 to 10,000 feet.
Special attractions: Access to Table Mountain from the west.
Water: Springs.
Best season: Summer through fall.
For more information: Toiyabe National Forest, Tonopah Ranger District, P.O. Box 3940, Tonopah, NV 89049-3940; (702) 482-6286.
Permit: None.

Finding the trailhead: From Tonopah, drive east six miles on U.S. Highway 6 and then turn north on Nevada Highway 376. After about thirteen miles turn northeast (right) on the Monitor Valley road, which is paved but eventually turns to graded dirt after Belmont. Continue on this road 45.3 miles. Turn right (northeast) at the signed, graded Morgan Creek-Mosquito Creek road and continue 5.7 miles; then turn right (east) on the Mosquito Creek road (FR 096). Go 0.5 miles then turn left on Forest Road 096A. This road goes one mile to the North Mosquito Creek trailhead, but it is washed out (a four wheel drive high clearance vehicle is required) and it may be preferable to park here or at the Mosquito Creek trailhead one mile up the main road.

The hike: Follow Forest Road 069A to the crest of a small hill. The trail takes off behind a wilderness boundary sign; initially it goes through a field of flat rock and is hard to follow for about 0.5 mile. After the trail drops off into the creek bottom, it is in a very pretty canyon; the trail follows this canyon to the top of Table Mountain. This trail could be used for a short traverse of the north end of the mountain, exiting at Morgan Creek. Alter-

The climax of the Toquima Range is the 11,000-foot Mount Jefferson plateau, seen here from FS Trail 44 in the Monitor Range. Views of mountains more than one hundred miles away are possible in Nevada's crystal clear air.

natively, a much longer, loop trip could be done with the Mosquito Creek or South Mosquito Creek Trails.—*USDA Forest Service and Bruce Grubbs*

HIKE 45 *SOUTH MOSQUITO CREEK TRAIL*

General description: A two- or three-day backpack trip in the Monitor Range.
General location: 70 miles northeast of Tonopah.
Maps: Green Monster Canyon 7.5-minute, Barley Creek 7.5-minute, Mosquito Creek 7.5-minute USGS, Toiyabe National Forest (Tonopah Ranger District) USDAFS.
Difficulty: Difficult.
Length: 13 miles one way.
Elevation: 7,150 to 9,900 feet.
Special attractions: Seldom used trail.
Water: Springs near Table Mountain.
Best season: Summer through fall.
For more information: Toiyabe National Forest, Tonopah Ranger District, P.O. Box 3940, Tonopah, NV 89049-3940; (702) 482-6286.
Permit: None.

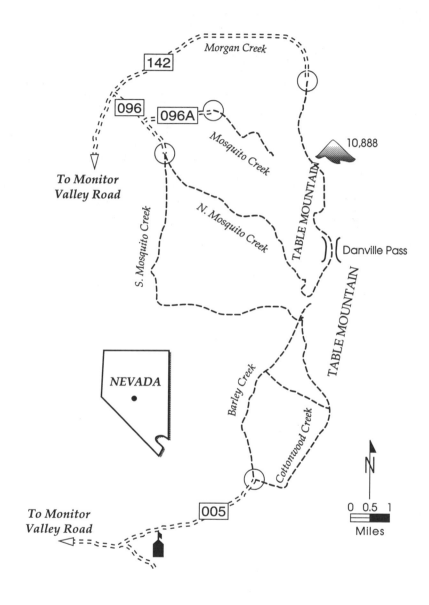

Finding the trailhead: From Tonopah, drive east six miles on U.S. Highway 6 then turn north on Nevada Highway 376. After about thirteen miles, turn east (right) on the paved Monitor Valley road, which turns to graded dirt after Belmont. Continue on this road 45.3 miles. Turn right (northeast) at the signed, graded Morgan Creek-Mosquito Creek road and continue 5.7 miles, then turn right (east) on the Mosquito Creek road (Forest Road 096). Go 2.1 miles to the Mosquito Creek trailhead, which is signed.

The hike: Start by following the unsigned Mosquito Creek trail south, across the creek from the parking area. The trail goes up a short steep section, and then the South Mosquito Creek Trail branches right (south) at an unsigned junction. It follows the South Fork of Mosquito Creek for a little more than a mile. Still heading south, it then follows a minor drainage over a saddle. From there it stays on a bench to the west for another mile before rejoining the South Fork. About two miles farther south, the South Fork and the trail both veer east. After a mile the, trail leaves the South Fork to the east and goes about a mile on the slopes northeast of the drainage before descending to cross the head of the South Fork. The trail climbs a ridge to the east and then crosses the head of Barley Creek before making the final climb to the gentle slopes of Table Mountain. Here the trail turns north to meet the Mosquito Creek trail in two miles.

It is possible to use this trail and the Mosquito Creek trail to do a loop over Table Mountain. The loop should start with the South Mosquito Creek Trail since it is harder to find than the Mosquito Creek Trail. That way, if the trail is lost you can return to the trailhead the way you came.—*USDA Forest Service and Bruce Grubbs*

HIKE 46 *COTTONWOOD CREEK-BARLEY CREEK TRAIL*

General description: A day hike in the Monitor Range.
General location: 62 miles northeast of Tonopah.
Maps: Barley Creek 7.5-minute, Green Monster Canyon 7.5-minute USGS, Toiyabe National Forest (Tonopah Ranger District) USDAFS.
Difficulty: Moderate.
Length: 10-mile loop.
Elevation: 7,700 to 9,370 feet.
Special attractions: Good trail giving access to Table Mountain from the south.
Water: Barley Creek, springs.
Best season: Summer through fall.
For more information: Toiyabe National Forest, Tonopah Ranger District, P.O. Box 3940, Tonopah, NV 89049-3940; (702) 482-6286.
Permit: None.

Finding the trailhead: From Tonopah, drive east six miles on U.S. Highway 6 then turn north on Nevada Highway 376. After about thirteen miles, turn northeast (right) on the Monitor Valley road, which is paved to Belmont; from there it is graded dirt. Continue on this maintained road 33.3 miles then turn

During the fall, sections of the Cottonwood Creek Trail in the Monitor Range are a golden tunnel through aspen groves. Yellow and orange leaves tremble on the trees, and the slightest breeze fills the air with the bright swirl of falling leaves.

The Barley Creek Trail is one of the most popular access routes to Table Mountain in the Monitor Range. It is especially popular with horse parties. Barley Creek has less water than Cottonwood Creek and so has less aspen and cottonwood trees. Most of the stream course is heavily lined with willow.

right on the Barley Creek road (Forest Road 093) and continue 6.2 miles to the signed Barley Creek turnoff (just past the Barley Creek Ranch). Turn left on the Barley Creek-Cottonwood Creek Road (FR 093) and continue four miles to the Cottonwood-Barley trailhead and the end of the road.

The hike: Go east on the Cottonwood Creek Trail (signed just beyond the trailhead). The well-built trail stays on the north side of the creek for a while. At first, the creek is lined only with willow, but soon you come to the first grove of aspen. In the fall, these graceful trees turn yellow and orange, adding colorful accents to the grey-green canyon.

One mile from the trailhead, there is a signed junction with the Willow Creek Trail. Stay on the Cottonwood Creek Trail as the creek turns north. The next mile features rugged cliffs on the west side of the canyon. Shortly after this section, there is a view of the south rim of Table Mountain, four miles to the north.

The trail crosses the little creek many times. Along the creek you will see western chokecherry, named because its astringent berries are impossible to eat. This broadleafed shrub has elliptical, finely toothed leaves that turn red-orange in the fall.

About 3.5 miles from the trailhead, watch for a signed junction with Trail #44 (the sign says "Barley Creek 3 mi"). Turn left (west) on this trail. It climbs steeply up a side canyon, veering north to switchback up to a ridge. It then crosses a saddle to the west, where there is a fine view of Mount Jefferson in the Toquima Range. Now Trail #44 descends into the broad valley below, staying on the north side of the drainage. Some sections of this trail are faint, but it is marked by large rock cairns. About three miles from the junction, the trail ends at a signed junction with the Barley Creek Trail.

Turn left (south) and follow the well-used trail down Barley Creek. This trail is a popular access to Table Mountain, especially for horse packers. For some reason Barley Creek has a lower flow than Cottonwood Creek, and the aspens are absent. The stream course is choked with willow, and the trail crosses it many times. There is a stand of narrowleaf cottonwood about a mile below the junction. Also known as black cottonwood, these water-loving trees are distinguished from the more common Fremont cottonwood by their narrow, willow-like leaves. The leaves of the Fremont cottonwood are triangular and often wider than they are long.

After 3.5 miles, you'll reach the trailhead, completing the loop. Both the Cottonwood and Barley trails can be used to reach Table Mountain, with the possibility of one-way hikes over the top. This would require a car shuttle to the Mosquito Creek or Morgan Creek trailheads.

HIKE 47 GREEN MONSTER TRAIL

General description: A day hike or overnight backpack in the Monitor Range.
General location: 81 miles northeast of Tonopah.
Maps: Green Monster Canyon 7.5-minute, Danville 7.5-minute USGS, Toiyabe National Forest (Tonopah Ranger District) USDAFS.
Difficulty: Difficult.
Length: 6 miles one way.
Elevation: 7,800 to 10,200 feet.
Special attractions: Access to Table Mountain from the east.
Water: Green Monster Creek.
Best season: Summer through fall.
For more information: Toiyabe National Forest, Tonopah Ranger District, P.O. Box 3940, Tonopah, NV 89049-3940; (702) 482-6286.
Permit: None.

Finding the trailhead: From Tonopah drive east 34.4 miles on U.S. Highway 6 then turn north on the Little Fish Lake Valley road (Forest Road 139). Where the road passes a dry lake bed called Squaw Flat, there is an impressive section of old roadway that was built by hand. Continue 43.8 miles then turn left (west) on the unsigned, unmaintained Green Monster road.

This turnoff is just north of a junction along the Little Fish Valley Lake road, where a signed right turn goes to Little Fish Valley Ranch (Forest Road 139 goes left). Stay right and drive 4.3 miles to the trailhead. This road can be driven by passenger cars with care. At the trailhead, two jeep roads branch right just before the main road crosses the creek to the south. Just after the crossing, a closed jeep road turns right, paralleling the creek. This is the unsigned Green Monster Trail. Camping is very limited near the trailhead; there is better camping several miles east along the access road.

The ruins of Wagon Johnnies Ranch on the road to Green Monster Canyon Trail in the Monitor Range. Old homesteads like this one are common in the canyons draining the mountain ranges. Many of the canyons have permanent streams, and provide some relief from the summer heat and protection from winter storms, but farming is usually difficult.

The hike: The old road parallels the creek for about 0.25 miles and then crosses to the north side. It passes through pleasant pinon-juniper woodland. The singleleaf pinon that grows here is easily identified since it is the only pine with its needles growing singly instead of in bunches of two or more. The nuts produced by this tree were highly prized by the natives as a food source, and are still valuable today. They are also an important staple for wildlife, especially woodrats.

About 0.5 miles from the trailhead, the jeep track ends abruptly, and the foot trail crosses to the south side of the creek again. It stays on the south side for about 0.25 mile, then crosses to the north side and remains there. There are few signs of trail maintenance, and the trail is confused by the cattle trails along the creek. After passing a fine stand of aspen, the trail crosses the creek to the south but only remains there a few yards before crossing again. At this point, a side canyon comes in from the southwest, but the trail continues up the fork to the west, the main creek. The trail climbs more steeply after this side canyon, which is about 1.5 mile from the trailhead; this makes a good stopping point for an easy day hike.

According to the Forest Service, the Green Monster Trail continues to Table Mountain where it connects to the Barley Creek and Cottonwood Creek trails. The origin of the name ''Green Monster'' is unknown, but probably an interesting story lies behind it.—*USDA Forest Service and Bruce Grubbs*

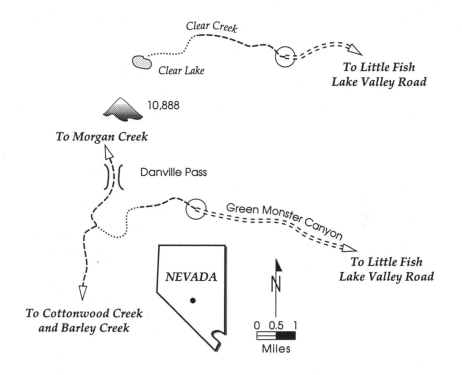

Clear Creek

Clear Lake

*To Little Fish
Lake Valley Road*

10,888

To Morgan Creek

Danville Pass

Green Monster Canyon

NEVADA

N

*To Little Fish
Lake Valley Road*

*To Cottonwood Creek
and Barley Creek*

0 0.5 1

Miles

HIKE 48 *CLEAR LAKE TRAIL*

General description: A day hike in the Monitor Range.
General location: 87 miles northeast of Tonopah.
Maps: Danville 7.5-minute USGS, Toiyabe National Forest (Tonopah Ranger District) USDAFS.
Difficulty: Moderate.
Length: 3 miles one way.
Elevation: 7,400 to 8,200 feet.
Special attractions: Aspen-filled canyon bottom, and access to the country east of Table Mountain.
Water: Lower Clear Creek near the trailhead and also near the end of the hike.
Best season: Summer through fall.
For more information: Toiyabe National Forest, Tonopah Ranger District, P.O. Box 3940, Tonopah, NV 89049-3940; (702) 482-6286.
Permit: None.

Finding the trailhead: From Tonopah, drive east 34.4 miles on U.S. Highway 6 then turn north on the Little Fish Lake Valley road. Continue 51.1 miles and then turn left on the signed Clear Lake road. This junction has four roads and is just after a cattleguard; the Clear Creek road goes west. Continue 2.1 miles to the end of the road. There are several campsites near the end of the road. The last 0.2 miles is more of a jeep track than a road, and is not worth driving.

The hike: The unsigned trail initially follows the south side of Clear Creek, through an open area caused by an old fire. The first half mile of the trail avoids the willow-choked stream bed, but then it crosses to the north side. A section of the creek may be dry, but there is water farther up the trail. Massive limestone cliffs tower above the trail as it drops into the streambed to wind through shady groves of aspen. This section of the hike provides very enjoyable walking as the trail climbs gradually. About 2.5 miles from the trailhead, the trail emerges from the aspens, and the canyon begins to open out into a basin with views of Table Mountain to the west and southwest. The foot trail meets an old jeep trail coming in from the north, and crosses Clear Creek again. This marks the end of the hike. There is a good flow of water here and a few campsites.

More experienced hikers who have a topographic map may wish to continue the hike to Clear Lake. The map shows the trail continuing to Clear Lake up Clear Creek, which turns to the southwest about 0.2 miles beyond the jeep trail, but I found instead that the trail goes up a shallow drainage, following the jeep trail onto the slope above. Here the trail disappears into cattle trails amid the sage. Go west toward a patch of drab green mountain mahogany that covers the ridge between this point and Clear Creek, and you will encounter the trail again as it contours into Clear Creek. After another 0.5 mile, the trail disappears again in a maze of cattle trails. I stopped here, but Clear Lake should be reachable by walking cross country on either side of Clear Creek. Except in the mahogany thickets the slopes are open sage. This optional hike to the lake would add two miles one way.—*USDA Forest Service and Bruce Grubbs*

A bird's nest in a young aspen stand along Clear Creek in the Monitor Range. Dense stands of water-loving plants and trees grow along the mountain streams, providing rich, riparian habitat for a wide variety of animal life. Most hiking trails follow the streams as well, and the trees provide welcome relief from the desert sun.

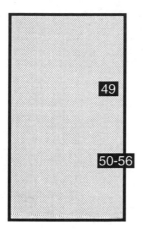

49. Hendrys Creek
50. Lehman Creek Trail
51. Wheeler Peak
52. Alpine Lakes Loop Trail
53. Bristlecone/Icefield Trail
54. Baker Creek Trail
55. Johnson Lake Trail
56. Lexington Arch Trail

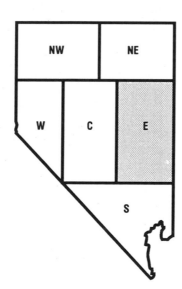

HIKE 49 *HENDRYS CREEK*

General description: A long day hike or overnight backpack trip in the Snake Range.

General location: 80 miles east of Ely.

Maps: Mount Moriah 7.5-minute, Old Mans Canyon 7.5-minute, The Cove 7.5-minute USGS; Humboldt National Forest (Ely Ranger District) USDAFS.

Difficulty: Difficult.

Length: 7 miles one way.

Elevation: 6,000 to 9,100 feet.

Special attractions: Scenic canyon, large aspen groves, access to "The Table" and Mount Moriah.

Water: Hendrys Creek.

Best season: Summer through fall.

For more information: Humboldt National Forest, Ely Ranger District, 350 E. 8th, P.O. Box 539, Ely, NV 89301; (702) 289-3031.

Permit: None.

Finding the trailhead: From Ely go east fifty-eight miles on U.S. Highways 6-50 to the junction of US 6-50 and Nevada Highway 487 (the highway to Baker and Great Basin National Park). The following mileages are from the "Y" Cafe at the junction.

Continue 0.2 miles east on US 6-50 then turn left (north) on an unsigned gravel road for 10.7 miles to a well-graded road coming from the right. Less than 0.1 miles before the junction, a rock cairn signed "Hatch Rock" marks a graded dirt road going left (northwest). Take this road 2.9 miles through a gate and past a "Hatch Rock Co." sign. Continue and watch for Forest Service "Trailhead" signs. Follow these signs ignoring any side roads. A sign marks the national forest boundary; park 0.1 miles farther at an obvious parking area, 14.7 miles from the Y Cafe. A sign points out the Hendrys Creek Trail.

The hike: The first two to three miles of trail follows an old road, which is severely washed out but has received Forest Service trail maintenance. The Mount Moriah Wilderness Area, established in 1989, is reached 1.5 miles from the trailhead. At 5.5 miles there is a signed junction with the Silver Creek Trail. Stay on the main trail, which becomes obscure in a few places. If in doubt, remain in the main drainage. Here the trail goes through continuous aspen groves. One and a half miles from the Silver Creek Trail junction the trail comes to a meadow bordered on three sides with aspen and good camping. To the west are views of the south side of Mount Moriah, and there are spectacular views down Hendrys Creek canyon. Beyond this meadow, Hendrys Creek forks several times, and the trail becomes consistently difficult to follow.

This point can be used as a base for hikes to "The Table," an 11,000-foot plateau, or to Mount Moriah (12,050 feet).—*Ron Kezar*

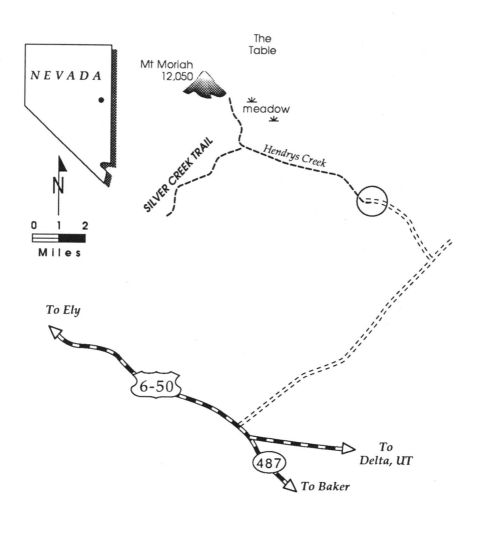

A number of ice-age glaciers carved the classic terrain of the Snake Range, leaving behind such features as the imposing Wheeler Cirque shown here, as well as numerous small alpine lakes. All of the ice is gone now, except for the Wheeler Icefield, which is the only permanent ice between the Sierra Nevada of California and the Wasatch Range of Utah. Stewart Aitchison photo.

125

HIKE 50 LEHMAN CREEK TRAIL

General description: A day hike in the Snake Range.
General location: 9 miles west of Baker.
Maps: Windy Peak 7.5-minute USGS.
Difficulty: Difficult.
Length: 4 miles one way.
Elevation: 7,800 to 9,950 feet.
Special attractions: A walk along scenic Lehman Creek.
Water: Lehman Creek.
Best season: Summer and fall.
For more information: Great Basin National Park, Baker, NV 89311; (702) 234-7331.
Permit: None.

Finding the trailhead: From Baker, drive west five miles on the Great Basin National Park entrance road (Nevada Highway 488). Then turn right (north) on the Wheeler Peak Scenic Drive. After about 2.5 miles, the road passes Upper Lehman Creek Campground; this is the lower trailhead. Continue on to where the road ends at the Wheeler Peak Campground, which is the upper trailhead. If the limited parking at the campground is taken, then backtrack and park 0.5 mile before the end of the road at the Wheeler Summit Trailhead.

The hike: The Lehman Creek Trail connects the Upper Lehman Creek Campground with the Wheeler Peak Campground. Both of these campgrounds are located along the Wheeler Peak Scenic Drive, and this trail provides a hiker's alternative to the road. The most enjoyable way to do this hike is via a car shuttle or have a driver drop off the hiking party at the Wheeler Peak Campground and meet them at the Upper Lehman Creek Campground, which would make this an all downhill hike.

Lehman Creek and Lehman Caves are named after Absalom Lehman, a settler who arrived in the area in 1869. He established a fruit orchard adjacent to what is now the visitor center parking lot and began supplying apricots, pears, peaches, and apples to the booming mining towns in the area. Today, only eight trees survive, and they are being managed by the Park Service to preserve the unique genetic resource.

Great Basin National Park, Nevada's only national park, was established in 1986. It includes the former Lehman Caves National Monument, which was designated in 1922. The park was created to protect a representative section of the Great Basin, and includes desert sage flats as well as mountainous alpine areas.

Lehman Caves is one of the largest limestone solution caves in the west. Numerous underground passages through the limestone are decorated with beautiful and classic cave formations. Guided tours are offered daily along a 0.66-mile-long trail through the cave. The cave formed in the Pole Canyon limestone, which is of Cambrian age. Deposited in shallow tropical seas similar to the present Caribbean, the rocks are about 550 million years old. Other layers of sediments continued to accumulate, compressing the limestone and partially recrystallizing it. Several periods of mountain building, from about

The snow-dusted alpine slopes of Wheeler Peak in the Snake Range tower above the open meadows and luxuriant forest at the head of Lehman Creek, Great Basin National Park.

70 million to 15 million years ago, lifted the limestone into mountain ranges, fracturing it in the process. Water, melting from the mountain snow and ice, found its way into these joints and faults, and dissolved the limestone to form a network of caverns that followed the lines of weakness in the rock. As the ice ages ended and the climate became drier, less water flowed through the caverns and the water table dropped. With the interior of the cave now filled with air, the remaining water deposits minerals as it evaporates, creating the flowstone and dripstone present today.

Since the Great Basin is still new, as landscapes go, many faults are still active today. The rate of movement averages up to two inches per year. The trail on which the guided walks take place follows a fault that has moved in historic time, offering a rare chance to observe a fault from underground.— *National Park Service and Bruce Grubbs*

From 13,063-foot Wheeler Peak in the Snake Range, the desert basins lie more than 7,000 feet below.

HIKE 51 *WHEELER PEAK*

General description: A day hike to Nevada's highest mountain.
General location: 17 miles west of Baker, Nevada.
Maps: Wheeler Peak 7.5-minute, Windy Peak 7.5-minute USGS, NPS brochure.
Difficulty: Difficult.
Length: 4 miles one way.
Elevation: 10,160 to 13,063 feet.
Special attractions: Outstanding alpine views.
Water: Stella Lake near the start.
Best season: Summer and fall.
For more information: Great Basin National Park, Baker, NV 89311; (702) 234-7331.
Permit: None.

Finding the trailhead: From Baker drive west five miles on the Great Basin National Park entrance road (Nevada Highway 488) and turn right (north) on the Wheeler Peak Scenic Drive. The signed Summit Trailhead is 0.5 mile before the end of the road.

The hike: Initally, the trail contours west through stands of aspen along the southern slopes of Bald Mountain. Openings in the aspen stands provide outstanding views of Wheeler Peak. After one mile of easy hiking, the trail intersects with the signed Alpine Lakes Trail, which comes from Wheeler Peak

Stella Lake reflecting Wheeler Peak, the highest summit in the Snake Range. Stella and Teresa lakes are located on the Alpine Lakes Trail, which forms a loop hike from Wheeler Peak Campground in Great Basin National Park.

Campground. There is yet another signed intersection about one hundred yards farther to the west where the Alpine Lakes Trail continues south to Stella Lake. The Wheeler Peak Trail turns sharply right and starts climbing.

The trail ascends through a wide meadow before a long switchback climbs to the main crest; please do not cut the switchback as the alpine vegetation is very fragile. Continue along the traverse until you gain the ridgeline at an elevation of almost 11,000 feet. Stunted and gnarled limber pine and Englemann spruce indicate treeline. Views are commanding to the east and west. The clear waters of Stella Lake are visible 1,000 feet below to the east.

Climb south up the wide ridgeline over loose quartzite scree and rocks. At the 12,000-foot level, the trail passes rock piles used for windbreaks. The final 1,000-foot climb to the summit is steep. Stay on the trail unless it is snow covered. In this case, chose your route carefully. Do not proceed if a safe route cannot be located. The snow slopes can be icy, very slippery, and are located above high cliffs. The summit is a long ridgeline with the highest point located in the center, overlooking the valleys 7,000 feet below.

Trees and plants growing at the treeline must adapt to the arctic environment of strong wind and severe cold. The trees tend to form dense low mats for protection from the cold, in areas where snow drifts form. The snow banks provide insulation and protection from the abrading effect of wind driven snow crystals. The parts of the trees that rise above the drift level often lose the branches on the windward side, forming characteristic "flag" trees. Other plants such as phlox and sky pilot grow in small dense mats in sheltered areas among the rocks.—*National Park Service and Bruce Grubbs*

A mule deer buck near the Wheeler Peak Trail, Great Basin National Park.

HIKE 52 *ALPINE LAKES LOOP TRAIL*

General description: A hike past alpine lakes in the Snake Range.
General location: 17 miles west of Baker.
Maps: Windy Peak 7.5-minute USGS, NPS brochure.
Difficulty: Easy.
Length: 3-mile loop.
Elevation: 10,000 to 10,400 feet.
Special attractions: Ancient bristlecone pine forest, alpine lakes, close-up views of high peaks in the Snake Range.
Water: Stella and Teresa Lakes.
Best season: Summer and fall.
For more information: Great Basin National Park, Baker, NV 89311; (702) 234-7331.
Permit: None.

Finding the trailhead: From Baker, drive west five miles on the Great Basin National Park entrance road (Nevada Highway 488) and then turn right (north) on the signed, paved Wheeler Peak Scenic Drive. Continue twelve miles to the trailhead, which is just before the entrance to Wheeler Peak Campground. If this parking lot is full, use the Summit Trailhead, which you passed 0.5 miles back. Then follow the Wheeler Peak Trail about one mile to join the Alpine Lakes Trail. Doing this adds about one mile to the hike.

The hike: The left trail is the Bristlecone/Icefield Trail, and the right trail is the Alpine Lakes Trail (also called the Stella Lake Trail). It starts by climbing through Englemann spruce and subalpine fir forest to the north of a small creek, then switchbacks to the right through meadows bordered with bristlecone pine, limber pine and aspen. There are fine views of Wheeler Peak. About 0.4 mile from the trailhead there is a signed junction with the Wheeler Peak Trail (if you had to park at the Summit Trailhead, you would join the Alpine Lakes Trail here). In about one hundred yards, the signed Wheeler Peak Trail turns sharply right; continue straight ahead 0.1 mile to Stella Lake.

Stella Lake is a typical glacial lake formed in a cirque created by a glacier. The moving ice "grinds down at the heel" of the mountain, forming a depression in the floor of the steep-walled valley at its head. After the ice melts, a deep cold lake is often left behind. Erosion of the steep mountainsides above the lake gradually fills it in. Stella Lake is in the last stages of fill, so it is shallow and freezes almost solid in the winter.

The trail skirts Stella Lake on the left and then wanders through uneven terrain. A glacier once covered this area; when it melted, it dropped its mixed load of dirt, sand, rocks and boulders in a jumbled heap. Sometimes large blocks of ice are left behind and isolated from the retreating mass of the main glacier, and later melt to form kettle lakes in depressions in the moraine. There are a number of depressions along this section of the trail that could contain small lakes, but don't. This is probably because of the dryness of the climate.

After about 0.5 mile, the trail descends in a single switchback to Teresa Lake. The depth of Teresa Lake varies greatly, depending on the amount of snow melt. The trail skirts the lake on the left and then continues down the drainage

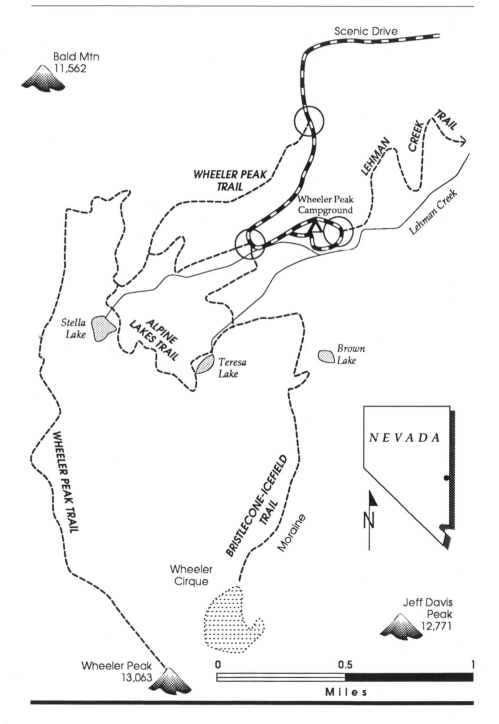

Scenic Drive

Bald Mtn
11,562

**WHEELER PEAK
TRAIL**

LEHMAN CREEK TRAIL

Wheeler Peak
Campground

Lehman Creek

Stella
Lake

**ALPINE
LAKES TRAIL**

Teresa
Lake

Brown
Lake

WHEELER PEAK TRAIL

BRISTLECONE-ICEFIELD TRAIL

Moraine

N E V A D A

N

Wheeler
Cirque

Jeff Davis
Peak
12,771

Wheeler Peak
13,063

0   0.5   1

M i l e s

below the lake. About 0.1 mile north of the lake, there is a signed junction with the Bristlecone-Icefield Trail.

This trail can be done as a side trip; it adds three miles to the trip. See Hike 53 Bristlecone-Icefield Trail for details.

The Alpine Lakes Trail continues straight ahead, downhill, and reaches the Wheeler Peak Campground trailhead in another 0.5 miles. If you parked at the Summit Trailhead, then turn left and use the start of the Alpine Lakes Trail to complete the loop.

HIKE 53 *BRISTLECONE-ICEFIELD TRAIL*

General description: A day hike to a glacial cirque in the Snake Range.
General location: 17 miles west of Baker.
Maps: Windy Peak 7.5-minute USGS, NPS brochure.
Difficulty: Moderate.
Length: 3 miles one way.
Elevation: 10,000 to 11,000 feet.
Special attractions: The Wheeler Icefield, which is the only permanent body of ice between the Sierra Nevada and the Wasatch Mountains, and a bristlecone pine interpretive trail.
Water: Teresa Lake.
Best season: Summer and fall.
For more information: Great Basin National Park, Baker, NV 89311; (702) 234-7331.
Permit: None. Backpackers are encouraged to register; no wood fires are allowed above 10,000 feet.

Finding the trailhead: From Baker, drive west five miles on the Great Basin National Park entrance road (Nevada Highway 488) and then turn right (north) on the signed, paved Wheeler Peak Scenic Drive. Continue twelve miles to the trailhead, which is just before the entrance to Wheeler Peak Campground. If this parking lot is full, use the Summit Trailhead, which you passed 0.5 mile back. Then follow the Wheeler Peak Trail about one mile to join the Alpine Lakes Trail, and then use the Alpine Lakes Trail to reach the Bristlecone Trail via Stella and Teresa lakes. Doing this adds about 3.5 miles to the hike.

The hike: From the Wheeler Peak Campground trailhead, take the left trail, which is signed Bristlecone-Icefield Trail. This trail climbs steadily for about 0.5 miles through dense limber pine and Englemann spruce forest and meets the Alpine Lakes Trail (Stella Lake Trail) at a signed junction. Turn left (east) and follow the Bristlecone-Icefield Trail as it first crosses over a low ridge and then climbs out across a shady north-facing slope. Where the trail turns right around the ridge, there is a good view of the upper Lehman Creek drainage and the Wheeler Peak Campground. Now the trail starts climbing gently along the slope, finally reaching the rough, jumbled terrain of the moraine left by the retreat of the Wheeler Glacier. There is a short, signed interpretive trail here that explains the bristlecone pines. It is worth the time and adds almost nothing to the hike distance.

This gnarled bristlecone pine is near the Bristlecone-Icefield Trail, Snake Range, Great Basin National Park. Bristlecone pines reach their greatest age on sites where the conditions are the most adverse. Trees growing in favorable, protected sites may reach an age of only a thousand years before succumbing to heartwood rot.

The Wheeler Icefield is the only permanent icefield in the vast Great Basin region between the Sierra Nevada and the Wasatch Mountains. Although it is not a true glacier, the icefield is an impressive sight, seen here from the end of the Bristlecone/Icefield Trail in the Snake Range, Great Basin National Park.

The bristlecone pine is a gnarled, tough tree of the timberline regions of the Southwest, and is easily recognized by its short, stiff needles growing five to a bundle; the branches resemble neat bottle brushes. Bristlecones are the oldest living things on Earth, reaching more than 6,000 years.

Tree ring dating is done without damaging the trees by screwing a slender cylinder into the heart of the tree. The cylinder is removed and the wood core extracted. Bands along the core are sections of the tree rings, and each ring represents a period of growth. Since bristlecones have one short period of growth each year, the rings may be counted and correlated with other tree ring data to accurately determine the tree's age, as well as indicate climate changes affecting the tree's growth rate. By correlating overlapping sections from older, and dead trees, the tree ring record has been extended back 10,000 years.

The two trails rejoin at a signed junction, and the trail continues up the moraine. The only trees that survive now are low mats of bristlecone pine, limber pine, and Englemann spruce. About 0.6 miles from the interpretive trail, the Bristlecone Trail ends at the foot of the Wheeler Icefield. In this stark canyon carved by ice and frost, life is reduced to a few hardy tundra plants growing in places where the rocks are stable. But even on the snow of the icefield there is life. In late summer you may notice a red stain on the old snow. This is caused by an algae that lives on snowfields.

Technically the Wheeler Icefield is not a glacier. Glaciers show valley movement, which causes their surfaces to break up into crevassed areas. An icefield, on the other hand, is relatively static. Enough snow falls each year to replace that lost to melting, but not enough to cause the icefield to expand.—*National Park Service and Bruce Grubbs*

Great Basin National Park is Nevada's first National Park and is intended to protect a typical cross section of Great Basin topography and wildlife. There are many hiking opportunities within the park. Stewart Aitchison photo.

HIKE 54 BAKER CREEK TRAIL

General description: A day hike in the Snake Range.

General location: 9 miles west of Baker.

Maps: Wheeler Peak 7.5-minute, Kious Spring 7.5-minute USGS, NPS brochure.

Difficulty: Difficult.

Length: 5 miles one way.

Elevation: 8,000 to 10,600 feet.

Special attractions: A hike along a mountain creek to a glacial lake in a rugged alpine setting.

Water: Baker Creek and Baker Lake.

Best season: Summer through fall.

For more information: Great Basin National Park, Baker, NV 89311; (702) 234-7331.

Permit: None. Backpackers are encouraged to register; no wood fires are allowed above 10,000 feet.

Finding the trailhead: From Nevada Highway 487 approximately five miles west of Baker, turn south on the Baker Creek road and continue to the end, 3.6 miles.

The hike: The Baker Lake Trail is signed and starts off in a steady climb along Baker Creek. It meanders through meadows and glades of aspen and subalpine fir for a while, passing a set of orange snow course markers. It then climbs the wide sage meadow north of the creek in a series of broad switchbacks. Note the contrast between the dry, south-facing slopes and the lush creek bottom. If you're doing this hike early in the morning after a clear, windless night, you'll be able to feel one of the reasons for the difference in vegetation. You'll notice that the air is much cooler near the creek than it is on the open sage slopes. This is because cool air from the mountains drains down the slopes at night, and collects in the valley bottoms. These microclimates support plant and animal communities adopted to the local conditions.

About a mile from the trailhead, there is an almost straight section of trail along the very edge of the aspen-fir forest. If you look closely at the aspens, you'll see that the leaves are trimmed off neatly about four feet above the ground. This is called a browse line, and it is caused by deer munching on the aspen up to a height they can comfortably reach.

More switchbacks follow, but the trail stays near the creek. Several small meadows lie along the trail; watch for a ponderosa pine in one of them. Ponderosa pines have three needles to the bunch, about four to six inches long, which gives the tree a bushier look than the other conifers. This ponderosa is very old and there are no young trees in the area, possibly indicating that ponderosa pine is on the way out in the Snake Range. These trees are very common in the Rocky Mountains but rare in Nevada. Another unusual plant found along the trail in patches on dry slopes. It is called manzanita, a low bush with characteristic red bark. Manzanita is abundant in central and southern Arizona and in southern California, but again rare in Nevada.

Baker Creek in Great Basin National Park near the trail to Baker Lake.

About 2.5 miles from the trailhead, you'll see another set of orange snow survey markers in a meadow below the trail. The Soil Conservation Service does the snow surveys, which are used to predict the amount of runoff during the spring snow melt. Since nearly all the water used in farms and cities in the west comes from the mountains, predicting the runoff is important. It is also used to predict the chances of flooding should sudden warm weather occur. The surveys were originally done on skis or snowshoes, and snow samples were taken to measure the snowpack's depth and density. Now, most of the survey work is done from aircraft. This snow survey marker is the type used by air observers.

About four miles from the trailhead, you'll pass the ruin of a sod-roofed log cabin. From here, the trail starts climbing in a series of wide, gentle switchbacks through an open forest of Englemann spruce and bristlecone pine. There are tantalizing glimpses of the high peaks. Finally, the trail rounds a low hill and Baker Lake comes into view. The glacial basin contains stands of timberline trees, and the steep cliffs above the lake complete the alpine setting.

A trail sign indicates the start of the trail to Johnson Lake over the pass west of Pyramid Peak. As mentioned under the Johnson Lake Trail description, Hike 55, this trail could be used for a one way hike to Johnson Lake trailhead, which would require a car shuttle.

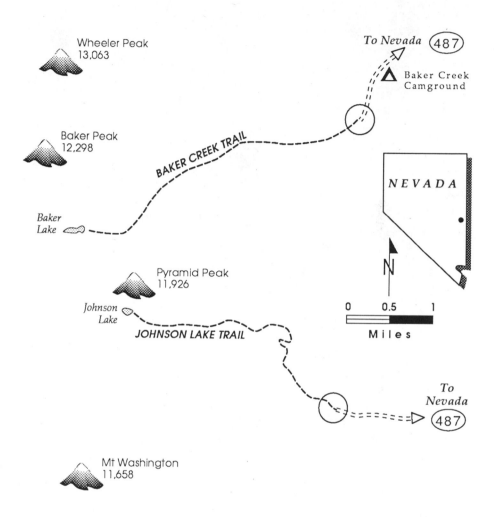

Wheeler Peak
13,063

To Nevada (487)

Baker Creek
Camground

Baker Peak
12,298

BAKER CREEK TRAIL

NEVADA

Baker
Lake

Pyramid Peak
11,926

Johnson
Lake

N

JOHNSON LAKE TRAIL

0   0.5   1

M i l e s

*To
Nevada*
(487)

Mt Washington
11,658

Aspens lit by the afternoon sun are highlighted against a background of Englemann spruce and limber pine along the Johnson Lake Trail in Great Basin National Park. The Snake Range is in eastern Nevada, and its proximity to the Rocky Mountains has allowed many Rocky Mountain plants and animals to colonize.

HIKE 55 *JOHNSON LAKE TRAIL*

General description: A day hike in the Snake Range.
General location: 18 miles southwest of Baker.
Maps: Wheeler Peak 7.5-minute USGS.
Difficulty: Difficult.
Length: 4 miles one way.
Elevation: 8,300 to 10,800 feet.
Special attractions: Unique forest with a blend of trees from the Rocky Mountains and the Great Basin; alpine lake in a glacial cirque.
Water: Snake Creek, Johnson Lake.
Best season: Summer through fall.
For more information: Great Basin National Park, Baker, NV 89311; (702) 234-7331.
Permit: None. Backpackers are encouraged to register; no wood fires are allowed above 10,000 feet.

Finding the trailhead: From Baker, drive south on Nevada Highway 487 5.2 miles, and turn right (west) on the signed, graded Snake Creek Canyon road. Follow this road thirteen miles to its end. There are numerous primitive campsites along the road. Just before the end of the road, a jeep road goes left; stay on the main road. The trailhead has a primitive campground with picnic tables in a fine aspen grove surrounding Snake Creek.

The hike: The Johnson Lake Trail follows an old jeep trail, which is closed to vehicles. It is not not marked or maintained, so you should have the topographic map. Start from the upper end of the parking lot and follow the unsigned old road directly up the hill. After a few hundred yards, another jeep road comes in from the left; the trail turns right and crosses Snake Creek. It stays north of Snake Creek all the way to Johnson Lake. After crossing the creek, the trail parallels it on the right, climbing through alpine meadows bordered with aspen and subalpine fir.

The forest type in the Snake Range is well-represented along the Johnson Lake Trail. Great Basin trees such as curlleaf mountain mahogany and bristlecone pine grow next to Rocky Mountain subalpine fir and Englemann spruce. Douglas-fir is also common, as is limber pine. Along this section of the trail, you should be able to identify subalpine fir by its flat needles that will not roll in your fingers and its spongy, cork-like bark. The needles of Douglas-fir are similar, but the bark is gray and deeply furrowed. Limber pine has two to three inch long needles, growing three to a bunch; the limbs are very flexible, helping the tree to survive heavy alpine snow loads.

After 0.75 miles along the creek, the trail veers away to the north and descends to cross a drainage. It then climbs out onto a sage-covered slope, which it ascends in a couple of switchbacks. Notice the contrast between this dry south-facing slope, covered with sage and mountain mahogany, and the moist north-facing slope covered with fir and aspen that you just descended.

After the switchbacks, the trail climbs steeply through forest in which bristlecone pine start to appear. You will also see Englemann spruce, with needles that grow singly like the firs, but are square in cross section so that

Johnson Lake in Great Basin National Park is a true alpine tarn. It was created by an ice-age glacier that ground a depression at its source high in the Snake Range. After the ice melted, a deep cold lake filled the basin.

they roll easily between your fingers. The trail heads a minor drainage in the forest, and climbs onto a point where the forest takes on a decidedly more alpine appearance. There are a number of campsites here but normally no water. In another half mile, the trail passes an old cabin. The remains of gold sluicing equipment show that the cabin was used by miners. There are a few campsites here, and there is water in the creek. This is a more sheltered spot to camp than Johnson Lake, which is still a mile up the trail.

After the cabin the old road becomes rougher and steeper for about a half mile, then moderates a bit for the final climb to the lake. More cabins, one of them fairly elaborate, are located just below the lake. Various cut logs and rusty pieces of equipment are strewn around the cabins and the lake, indicating that a lot of activity took place here. There is even a cable strung from one of the mines high on the talus slope. Some of the cut timber might have been used to support a tramway. The lake itself is small, but the west end is deep. It is a true alpine tarn—a lake created by a glacier.

Although the trail is visible as it continues over the pass above the lake, this hike ends here. The trail over the pass goes to Baker Lake, and with a car shuttle it would be possible to visit Baker Lake and descend to the Baker Creek trailhead. See Hike 54 Baker Lake Trail, for more information.—*National Park Service and Bruce Grubbs*

HIKE 56 *LEXINGTON ARCH TRAIL*

General description: A round-trip day hike to a natural arch in the Snake Range.

General location: 24 miles southwest of Baker.

Maps: Arch Canyon 7.5-minute USGS, NPS brochure.

Difficulty: Moderate.

Length: 1 mile one way.

Elevation: 7,440 to 8,440 feet.

Special attractions: Natural arch, remote section of the park.

Water: None.

Best season: Summer.

For more information: Great Basin National Park, Baker, NV 89311; (702) 234-7331.

Finding the trailhead: From Baker drive 10.7 miles southeast on Nevada Highway 487 (the road becomes Utah Highway 21). Then turn right on the first dirt road past Pruess Lake. Proceed west twelve miles, following the signs for Lexington Arch. This road is unmanintained and a high-clearance vehicle is recommended. Please leave all gates as you find them, to help keep livestock on its proper range.

The hike: Although the trailhead is signed, the trail is sometimes obscure as it ascends its steep and rocky course. Once you reach the base of the arch, the trail swings around the left side of the arch. From here you can climb into the arch's opening.

Rising high above the floor of Lexington Canyon, this imposing natural arch was created by the forces of weather working slowly over a span of centuries. Lexington Arch is unusual in one important respect: it is carved from limestone. Most of the natural arches of the western United States are composed of sandstone. The fact that Lexington Arch is made of limestone leads to speculation that it was once a passage in a cave system. Flowstone, a smooth, glossy deposit that forms in caves, has been found at the base of the opening, lending support to this theory. It is even possible that Lexington Arch is actually a natural bridge. The distinction: an arch is formed by the forces of weathering, such as ice, wind, and chemical breakdown of the rock. A natural bridge, by contrast, is formed by the flowing waters of a stream. It is possible that long ago when Lexington canyon was less deep, the waters of Lexington Creek flowed through a cave in the wall of the canyon, in the process enlarging the tunnel that later became Lexington Arch. If this happened then the "arch" is truly a bridge.—
National Park Service

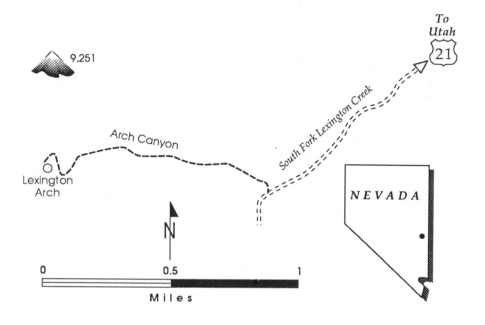

SOUTHERN NEVADA

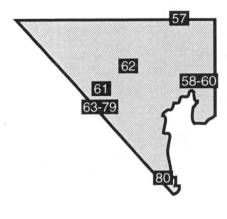

57. Cathedral Gorge
58. Mouse's Tank
59. Fire Canyon—Silica Dome
60. White Domes
61. Charleston Peak National Scenic Trail
62. Joe May Canyon
63. Moenkopi Trail
64. Calico Hills
65. Calico Tanks
66. Turtlehead Peak
67. Keystone Thrust
68. White Rock Hills
69. White Rock Spring
70. White Rock Spring to Willow Spring
71. Lost Creek Loop
72. Willow Spring Loop
73. La Madre Spring
74. Top of the Escarpment
75. Bridge Mountain
76. Ice Box Canyon
77. Pine Creek Canyon
78. Oak Creek Canyon
79. First Creek Canyon
80. Spirit Peak

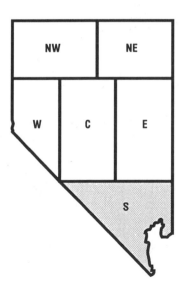

HIKE 57 _CATHEDRAL GORGE_

General description: A day hike in Cathedral Gorge State Park.
General location: 15 miles north of Caliente.
Maps: Panaca 7.5-minute USGS.
Difficulty: Easy.
Length: Approximate 5-mile loop.
Elevation: 5,000 feet.
Special attractions: Badland erosional forms.
Water: At campground.
Best season: Spring and fall.
For more information: Nevada Division of State Parks, 4747 Vegas Dr., Las Vegas, NV 89108; (702) 486-5126.
Permit: None.

Finding the trailhead: From Caliente, drive north on U.S. Highway 93 for fifteen miles to the signed turnoff for Cathedral Gorge State Park.

The hike: The main trail starts from the campground and loops through Cathedral Gorge, returning to the picnic area via a one-mile trail connecting the picnic area with Miller Point Overlook. Shorter trails connect the picnic areas together, and the access road may be used to return to the campground, completing the loop.

The buff-colored rocks of Cathedral Gorge are remnants of a lake bed dating from about one million years ago. Then, much of Meadow Valley was covered by a freshwater lake. Sediments accumulated on the bottom as streams and washes brought eroded material into the lake. As the climate gradually became more arid, the lake dried up and the siltstone and clay of the Panaca formation were eroded into the present shapes. Clay erodes into typical "badlands," with steep barren slopes changing abruptly to equally barren flats.

Erosion proceeds rapidly allowing few plants to grow. Sand dunes are also hostile environments, but plants such as dune primroses and Indian rice grass may gain a foothold and act to stabilize the sand. In the valley, clay, sand, and gravel have mixed to form a more hospitable soil that supports narrowleaf yucca, junipers, barberry, greasewood, and of course the ubiquitous sagebrush.

Jack rabbits and cottontail rabbits are common as are coyotes, kit foxes, skunks, packrats, kangaroo rats, mice, and gophers. Deer also are seen around Miller Point. Nonpoisonous lizards and snakes are common, and the Great Basin rattlesnake may be found during warm weather. Resident birds you may see include ravens, kestrals and small hawks, roadrunners, sapsuckers, robins, black-throated sparrows, finches, blackbirds, and starlings. Tanagers, cedar waxwings, warblers, bluebirds, and hummingbirds migrate through the Park area in the spring and fall.—_Nevada Division of State Parks_

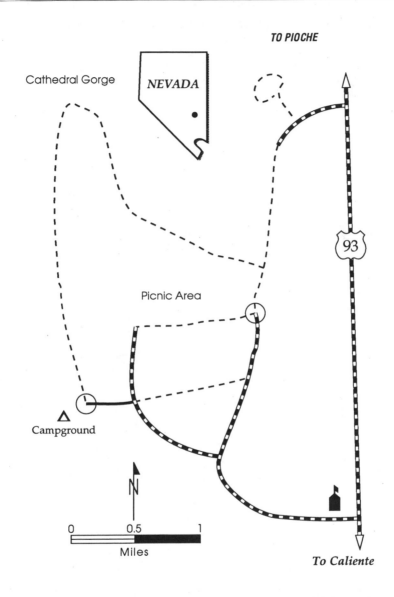

HIKE 58 _MOUSE'S TANK_

General description: A day hike in Valley of Fire State Park.
General location: 55 miles northeast of Las Vegas.
Maps: Valley of Fire East 7.5-minute, Valley of Fire West 7.5-minute USGS.
Difficulty: Easy.
Length: 0.3 mile one way.
Elevation: 2,000 feet.
Special attractions: Interpretive trail, petroglyphs and natural water tanks.
Water: None.
Best season: Fall through spring.
For more information: Nevada Division of State Parks, 4747 Vegas Dr., Las Vegas, NV 89108; (702) 486-5126.
Permit: None.

Finding the trailhead: From Las Vegas drive northeast on Interstate 15 approximately fifty-five miles then turn right on Nevada Highway 169, which is signed for Valley of Fire State Park. Continue into the park and turn left at the visitor center, about eighteen miles from I-15. After 0.2 miles turn left (before reaching the visitor center) and continue about one mile to the signed Mouse's Tank parking area on the right.

The hike: The trail follows Petroglyph Canyon east from the parking area. Brochures are available at the trailhead explaining various features along this

Petroglyphs in Petroglyph Canyon on the walk to Mouse's Tank, Valley of Fire State Park. Petroglyphs are often confused with pictographs. Petroglyphs are ancient art work carved into the stone, while pictographs are ancient art work painted onto the surface of the rock.

Mouse's Tank in the Valley of Fire State Park was a valuable but well-hidden water source.

short walk. It points out a couple of petroglyphs along the way, but sharp-eyed hikers will see several more. After a relatively straight section, the wash veers sharply left, and in a few dozen yards drops into the first of several natural water tanks. This water may seem stagnant and uninviting (and is not presently safe to drink), but it would become infinitely more valuable if one was on foot many miles from civilization.

In 1897, Mouse, a Paiute Indian who was suspected of several crimes, hid out in the intricate Valley of Fire area to avoid capture. He used this water tank and probably others to survive in this nearly waterless area.

The striking red rocks of the Valley of Fire are the Aztec sandstone, which is composed of petrified sand dunes. Tiny grains of wind blown sand make up the rock, and the sloping surfaces of the ancient sand dunes are clearly visible in the rock faces along the trail. The forces of erosion, primarily that of water, have acted over millions of years to sculpt the soft rock into the weird shapes found in the park.

HIKE 59 *FIRE CANYON—SILICA DOME*

General description: A day hike in Valley of Fire State Park.
General location: 55 miles northeast of Las Vegas.
Maps: Valley of Fire East 7.5-minute, Valley of Fire West 7.5-minute USGS.
Difficulty: Easy.
Length: 1 mile one way.
Elevation: 2,000 feet.
Special attractions: Excellent view of Fire Canyon and Silica Dome.
Water: None.
Best season: Fall through spring.
For more information: Nevada Division of State Parks, 4747 Vegas Dr., Las Vegas, NV 89108; (702) 486-5126.
Permit: None.

Finding the trailhead: From Las Vegas drive northeast on Interstate 15 approximately fifty-five miles and then turn right on Nevada Highway 169, which is signed for Valley of Fire State Park. Continue into the park and turn left at the visitor center, about eighteen miles from I-15. After 0.2 miles turn left (before reaching the visitor center) and continue about 1.5 miles to the end of the paved road.

The hike: The unsigned trailhead is at the north end of the parking lot, marked by "No Parking" and "Road Closed" signs. The trail follows an old road, a former scenic drive that is now closed to motorized vehicles. Several hundred yards from the trailhead, the White Dome Trail (signed) branches left. Continue straight ahead (east) about 0.9 mile to the viewpoint on the unsigned Fire Canyon Trail.

The superb view reveals many interesting things about the landscape. The Virgin Mountains on the Arizona-Nevada state line are visible thirty miles to the northeast. These 8,000-foot mountains often have snow during the winter. Forty miles to the northwest, the 10,000-foot Sheep Creek Range dominates the distant skyline, with the White Domes area forming the middle distance. To the south, the domes and canyons of Fire Canyon shade from white to red, with the somber gray tones of the Muddy Mountains forming the skyline about five miles away.

The Muddy Mountains are made up of limestone that is much older than the sandstone in the Valley of Fire. Normally younger rocks are found on top of older rocks, because the layers are deposited in sequence. But here the older limestone was once on top of the sandstone. This was caused by thrust faulting during the building of the North American continent in which the limestone was forced many miles over the top of the sandstone.

HIKE 60 *WHITE DOMES*

General description: A day hike in Valley of Fire State Park.
General location: 55 miles northeast of Las Vegas.
Maps: Valley of Fire East 7.5-minute, Valley of Fire West 7.5-minute USGS.
Difficulty: Easy.
Length: 3.5 miles one way.
Elevation: 2,000 to 2,200 feet.
Special attractions: Access to primitive northern area of park.
Water: None.
Best season: Fall through spring.
For more information: Nevada Division of State Parks, 4747 Vegas Dr., Las Vegas, NV 89108; (702) 486-5126.
Permit: None.

Finding the trailhead: Follow the directions for Hike 59 Fire Canyon-Silica Dome. The unsigned trailhead is at the north end of the parking lot, marked by "No Parking" and "Road Closed" signs.

The hike: The trail follows an old road, a former scenic drive that is now closed to motorized vehicles. Several hundred yards from the trailhead, the signed White Dome Trail branches left. Ahead, the old road can be seen winding through the desert amid outcrops of sandstone. The view to the north and northeast is excellent.

The trail ends in the White Dome area. Note the nearly white sandstone in this area, in contrast to the deep red sandstone near the visitor center. The red color in the rock is caused by traces of iron minerals that have oxidized, or literally rusted. Subtle changes in the colors, from white to tan, purple, maroon and red are thought to be caused by underground water movement which leached the oxidized iron.

Many believe that wind erodes desert landscapes such as this one. However, wind plays a minor part, mainly moving loose sand and heaping it into small sand dunes. Water is actually responsible for most of the landforms within the park. That seems fantastic in this arid landscape, especially if one has only seen the rare and gentle winter rains. But every few years the area is subjected to heavy rains from strong summer thunderstorms, and even more rarely, prolonged winter rain like the two-week rain of January 1993. The power of water becomes more apparent when one multiplies the effects of one of these storms by millions of storms occurring over many millions of years.

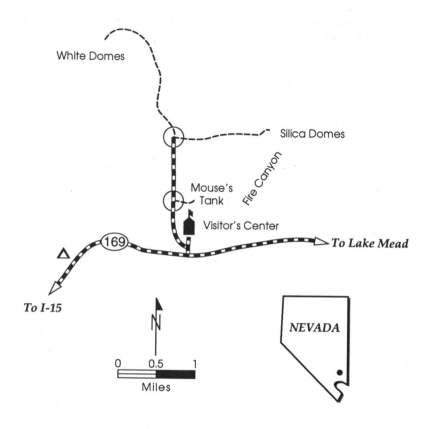

White Domes

Silica Domes

Fire Canyon

Mouse's Tank

Visitor's Center

To Lake Mead

169

To I-15

N

0   0.5   1
Miles

NEVADA

HIKE 61 *CHARLESTON PEAK NATIONAL SCENIC TRAIL*

General description: A day hike in the Spring Mountains.

General location: Approximately 49 miles northwest of Las Vegas.

Maps: Charleston Peak 7.5-minute USGS; Toiyabe National Forest (Las Vegas Ranger District) USDAFS.

Difficulty: Difficult.

Length: 13-mile loop.

Elevation: 7,700 to 11,918 feet.

Special attractions: High ridge hike with spectacular alpine views.

Water: Spring on Mummy Mountain.

Best season: Summer through fall.

For more information: Toiyabe National Forest, Las Vegas Ranger District, 2881 S. Valley View, Suite 16, Las Vegas, NV 89104; (702) 873-8800.

Permit: None.

Special instructions: Caution should be used if attempting this hike in late spring or early summer as the higher sections of the trail may be covered with snow, especially the North Loop near Charleston Peak. It may not be possible to traverse the steep slopes safely without technical climbing equipment and experience.

Finding the trailhead: From Las Vegas drive northwest on U.S. Highway 95 about thirteen miles and turn left (west) on the signed and paved Kyle Canyon Road, Nevada Highway 157. Continue nineteen miles to the summer home area then continue straight on Echo Road (NV 157 turns sharply left and crosses the creek). After 0.5 mile turn right (staying on Echo Road) and go 0.1 mile to the North Loop trail head.

The loop hike ends at the South Loop trailhead, 1.5 miles away. To drive to the South Loop Trailhead, stay on NV 157 to its end at the Cathedral Rock Picnic Area; the trailhead is within the picnic area and is signed.

The hike: The North Loop Trail climbs steeply up a drainage as it heads toward the crest of the range. A beautiful forest of ponderosa pine and quaking aspen gives way to a more open view in an old burn on the southwest slopes of Mummy Mountain. A series of switchbacks lead to the unsigned junction with the Deer Creek Trail in a saddle. Swinging northwest, the trail climbs across Mummy Mountain past the spring shown on the topographic map. After the spring, the trail swings southwest and west, gradually climbing to the crest where there are views of the Lee Canyon area to the north.

Staying near the crest but skirting minor peaks to the left, the trail traverses limestone slopes forested with bristlecone pine and finally reaches the east slope of Charleston Peak where the trail switchbacks upward to the summit.

The South Loop Trail descends the treeless west slopes of the peak from just north of the summit then follows the long, nearly level crest through a fine bristlecone forest. About 0.5 mile before reaching peak 11,072, the trail turns left (north) at the signed junction with the Lovell Canyon Trail, and descends via numerous switchbacks toward the floor of Kyle Canyon. Near the bottom, the trail drops into a drainage to avoid high limestone cliffs; this

The South Mount Charleston Loop Trail in the Spring Mountains provides excellent views, staying at 11,000 feet for more than six miles.

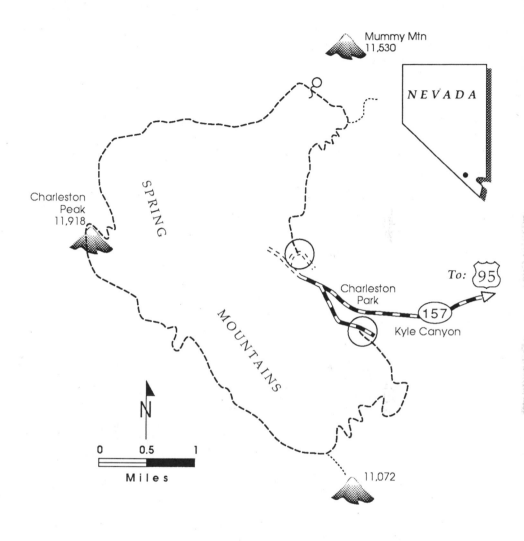

spectacular area is a major snow avalanche path in winter. Notice that there are few trees in the drainage, and the trees near the sides are all of the same size and age. This is due to the regular occurrence of snow slides that destroy the trees.

At the bottom of the drainage, there is a choice of a left and right fork; stay right on the newer trail. At the picnic area it is easy to walk up the road to the North Loop trailhead.

HIKE 62 *JOE MAY CANYON*

General description: A day hike in the Desert National Wildlife Range.
General location: Approximately 35 miles north of Las Vegas.
Maps: Black Hills 7.5-minute, Corn Creek Springs 7.5-minute USGS.
Difficulty: Moderate.
Length: 3.4 miles one way.
Elevation: 4,800 to 6,861 feet.
Special attractions: Good opportunity to observe bighorn sheep, including lambs.
Water: None.
Best season: March through May.
For more information: Desert National Wildlife Refuge, 1500 N. Decatur Blvd., Las Vegas, NV 89108; (702) 646-3401.
Permit: None.

Finding the trailhead: From Las Vegas drive northwest twenty miles on U.S. Highway 95 then turn right (east) on the Corn Creek Springs Road (this road is signed "Desert National Range"). After four miles turn left (north) onto Alamo Road at the Corn Creek Field Station. Drive north three miles then turn right (east) onto the Joe May Canyon Road and continue 3.7 miles to the proposed wilderness boundary, identified by a "No Vehicles" sign. The Joe May Canyon Road is unimproved and a high-clearance vehicle is recommended. Four wheel drive is not needed.

The Corn Creek Field Station, passed on the way to the trailhead, has an interesting history. It has seen use as a campsite, stagecoach stop, and ranch. Corn Creek Springs and part of the surrounding land was purchased in 1939 for use as a field station for the wildlife refuge. The station, with its trees, pasture, and spring-fed ponds, attracts a wide variety of migrating birds not commonly observed in such an arid environment. The ponds also provide habitat for the endangered Pahrump poolfish. Evidence of man's earlier occupation of this site is provided by Native American arrowhead and tool flakes that litter the surrounding grounds. Also of interest are the historical buildings located at the northern side of the field station.

The hike: Walk north up Joe May Canyon to Wildhorse Pass, which provides an excellent panoramic view into scenic Picture Canyon. About 1.5 miles from the "No Vehicles" sign is the Joe May Guzzler in a small side canyon. This is an example of one method used to develop water for bighorn sheep and other wildlife.

Desert bighorn sheep prefer rugged mountains and negotiate steep terrain with impressive agility for their somewhat bulky appearance. The size of a small deer, their gray brown color blends nicely with the desert tones, making them difficult to spot. Males are distinguished by their massive curling horns, while the females have much smaller horns. It is thought that the bighorns once ranged much more widely, but pressure from man has limited them to more rugged terrain. Although they cannot survive without liquid water, the sheep do obtain enough moisture from green vegetation to enable them to go without water three to five days in hot weather and ten to fourteen days

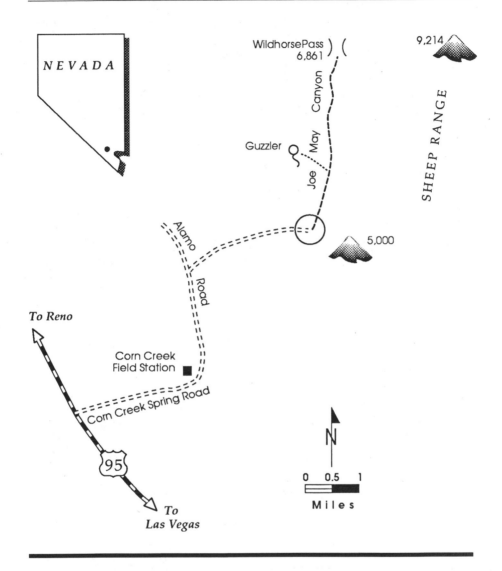

in cold weather. The east side of Joe May Canyon is an excellent lambing area and one may be able to observe large groups of ewes and lambs in this area. Good binoculars will be useful.—*USDA Fish and Wildlife Service and Bruce Grubbs*

HIKE 63 *MOENKOPI TRAIL*

General description: A day hike on an interpretive trail in the Red Rock Canyon National Conservation Area.

General location: Approximately 15 miles west of Las Vegas.

Maps: La Madre Mtn. 7.5-minute USGS.

Difficulty: Easy.

Length: 2-mile loop.

Elevation: 3,700 feet.

Special attractions: Triassic fossils and diverse desert plant communities.

Water: None.

Best season: Fall through spring.

For more information: Red Rock Canyon National Conservation Area, Bureau of Land Management, P.O. Box 26569, Las Vegas, NV 89126; (702) 363-1921.

Permit: None (day use only).

Finding the trailhead: From Las Vegas drive west on Charleston Blvd. (Nevada Highway 159) to reach the Red Rock Scenic Loop, approximately eleven miles from the intersection of Charleston and Rainbow boulevards. Turn right (north) on the Scenic Loop Road then left to the Bureau of Land Management Visitor Center. Here you can obtain general information on the Red Rock area and check on the road and trail conditions.

The 2,000-foot cliffs of the Red Rock Canyon National Conservation Area are composed of red and white layers of Aztec sandstone, rising dramatically above the older gray limestone forming the valley floor.

The hike: The Moenkopi Trail starts southwest of the visitor center near the weather station. Along the way watch for creosote, blackbrush, and yucca, which are typical members of this desert plant community. The trail leads to the crest of the hill west of the visitor center. At the crest, cottontop barrel cactus and Triassic fossils can be seen.

Creosote bush, found along this trail and common in southern Nevada and the rest of the Mohave Desert, is an outstanding example of the extreme methods desert plants use to survive drought. During dry periods, the bush sheds its mature leaves as well as whole twigs and branches, retaining only the new leaves. These leaves can lose well over half their water and still survive. In comparison, humans are seriously ill after a water loss of only a few percent.—*Bureau of Land Management and Bruce Grubbs*

HIKE 64 *CALICO HILLS*

General description: A day hike in the Red Rock Canyon National Conservation Area.
General location: Approximately 15 miles west of Las Vegas.
Maps: La Madre Mtn 7.5-minute USGS.
Difficulty: Easy.
Length: 1 mile one way.
Elevation: 3,920 to 4,329 feet.
Special attractions: Slickrock sandstone hills.
Water: None.
Best season: Fall through spring.
For more information: Red Rock Canyon National Conservation Area, Bureau of Land Management, P.O. Box 26569, Las Vegas, NV 89126; (702) 363-1921.
Permit: None (day use only).

Finding the trailhead: Follow the description for Hike 63 Moenkopi Trail to reach the Bureau of Land Management Visitor Center. Then continue on the loop road (one way) to either of the two Calico Hills overlooks.

The hike: Short trails lead from each overlook into the wash at the base of the Calico Hills. From the wash it is easy to scramble up the sandstone hills. This very easy walk gives one a quick idea of the nature of slickrock. Look for many seasonal pools found in the rock formations.

The origin and exact meaning of the term slickrock is unclear. It is generally used in the American Southwest to describe areas of exposed sandstone such as this. The term is descriptive, because in arid climates sandstone erodes to form sleekly rounded domes and turrets, which look slick from a distance. Up close, the hiker will discover that the rock is anything but slick. It is nature's sandpaper, composed of billions of grains of sand cemented together by heat and pressure. Contrary to popular opinion, slickrock country is primarily eroded by water during the rare desert storms. Wind plays a very minor role.—*Bureau of Land Management and Bruce Grubbs*

Slickrock sandstone forms a complex topography more typical of Utah in the Calico Hills, part of the Red Rock Canyon National Conservation Area near Las Vegas.

HIKE 65 *CALICO TANKS*

General description: A day hike in the Red Rock Canyon National Conservation Area.
General location: Approximately 15 miles west of Las Vegas.
Maps: La Madre Mtn. 7.5-minute USGS.
Difficulty: Easy.
Length: 0.3 mile one way.
Elevation: 4,800 feet.
Special attractions: Opportunity to observe bighorn sheep.
Water: None.
Best season: Fall through spring.
For more information: Red Rock Canyon National Conservation Area, Bureau of Land Management, P.O. Box 26569, Las Vegas, NV 89126; (702) 363-1921.
Permit: None (day use only).

Finding the trailhead: Follow the description for Hike 63 Moenkopi Trail to reach the Bureau of Land Management Visitor Center. Then continue on the loop road (one way) to the lower White Rock Springs parking area and turn right. Drive the dirt road 0.8 mile to its end and park.

The hike: The trail is a closed dirt road on the left (west). Follow the old road to the water catchment constructed by the Civilian Conservation Corps. This is a good place to observe bighorn sheep, in season.

Water catchments such as this one are intended to expand the range of the desert bighorn sheep by providing additional permanent water sources. This enables the animals to use more of their natural habitat.—*Bruce Grubbs and Bureau of Land Management*

HIKES 63, 64, 65, & 66

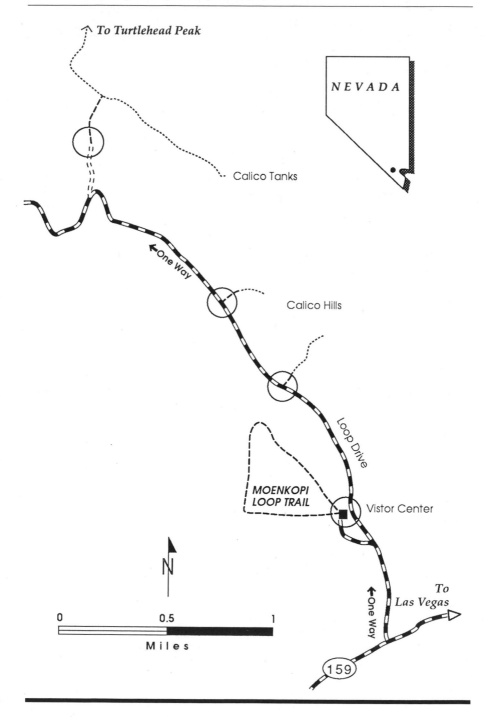

To Turtlehead Peak

NEVADA

Calico Tanks

One Way

Calico Hills

Loop Drive

MOENKOPI
LOOP TRAIL

Vistor Center

N

| 0 | 0.5 | 1 |

Miles

One Way

To
Las Vegas

159

HIKE 66 *TURTLEHEAD PEAK*

General description: A day hike in the Red Rock Canyon National Conservation Area.

General location: Approximately 15 miles west of Las Vegas. Maps: La Madre Mtn. 7.5-minute USGS, BLM brochure.

Difficulty: Difficult.

Length: 2.5 miles one-way.

Elevation: 4,280 to 6,324 feet.

Special attractions: Spectacular views.

Water: None.

Best season: Fall through spring.

For more information: Red Rock Canyon National Conservation Area, Bureau of Land Management, P.O. Box 26569, Las Vegas, NV 89126; (702) 363-1921.

Permit: None (day use only).

The hike: Follow the description for Hike 63 to reach the Bureau of Land Management Visitor Center. Then continue on the loop road (one way) to Sandstone Quarry and park. This route follows a wash north through the Calico Hills, climbs a revine to the left of Turtlehead, and follows the ridge to the top. The spectacular views are well worth the long climb.

From the summit, you can see a representative sample of the Mohave Desert, which encompasses the southern tip of Nevada, most of southeastern California, and a bit of western Arizona. The Mohave's symbol is the Joshua Tree, a large yucca. Joshua Trees tend to grow on the higher slopes of the valleys; creosote bush dominates lower elevations; a yucca belt is found at higher elevations, and above the yuccas, a pinyon life zone where the dominate plants are the pinyon pines and juniper trees.—*Bureau of Land Management and Bruce Grubbs*

HIKE 67 *KEYSTONE THRUST*

General description: A day hike in the Red Rock Canyon National Conservation Area.

General location: Approximately 15 miles west of Las Vegas.

Maps: La Madre Mtn. 7.5-minute USGS, BLM brochure.

Difficulty: Easy.

Length: 2 miles one-way.

Elevation: 4,800 to 5,300 feet.

Special attractions: Keystone Thrust Fault contact zone.

Water: None.

Best season: Fall through spring.

For more information: Red Rock Canyon Naitonal Conservation Area, Bureau of Land Management, P.O. Box 26569, Las Vegas, NV 89126; (702) 363-1921.

Permit: None (day use only).

The hike: Follow the description for Hike 63 Moenkopi Trail to reach the Bureau of Land Management Visitor Center. Then continue on the loop road (one way) to the lower White Rock Springs parking area and park. Follow the the dirt road 0.8 mile to a closed dirt road on the right (east). Follow the trail approximately 0.75 mile to the fork and follow the right fork down to the small canyon and the contact of the Keystone Thrust Fault.

A thrust fault is a fracture in the earth's crust where one rock plate is thrust horizontally over another. Normally younger rocks are found on top of older rocks, as they are deposited in layered succession. But here the older limestone has been pushed over the top of the younger sandstone. It is believed that this occurred about 65 million years ago when two continental plates collided to create the present North American continent. The thrust contact is clearly defined by the sharp contrast between the gray limestones and the red sandstones. The Keystone Thrust Fault extends from the Cottonwood Fault (along the Pahrump Highway) thirteen miles northward to the vicinity of La Madre Mountain where it is obscured by more complex faulting.—*Bureau of Land Management*

HIKE 68 *WHITE ROCK HILLS*

General description: A cross-country day hike in the Red Rock Canyon National Conservation Area.

General location: Approximately 15 miles west of Las Vegas.

Maps: La Madre Mtn 7.5-minute USGS.

Difficulty: Easy.

Length: 2 miles one way.

Elevation: 4,800 to 5,100 feet.

Special attractions: Dramatic view of La Madre Spring valley.

Water: None.

Best season: Fall through spring.

For more information: Red Rock Canyon Recreation Lands, Bureau of Land Management, P.O. Box 26569, Las Vegas, NV 89126; (702) 363-1921.

Permit: None (day use only).

Finding the trailhead: Follow the description for Hike 63 Moenkopi Trail to reach the Bureau of Land Management visitor center. Then continue on the loop road (one way) to the lower White Rock Spring parking area and turn right. Follow the dirt road 0.9 mile to its end and park.

The hike: Go west down a short closed road, which drops into the wash to the right of the White Rock Hills. Then continue up the wash along the base of the sandstone bluffs. After about 0.5 mile, a faint trail veers out of the wash to the right. A few cairns mark the route as it parallels the wash. About two miles from the trailhead, the route reaches a saddle with excellent views of the west side of the White Rock Hills and the valley above La Madre Spring. The towering limestone cliffs on the right make a somber contrast with the bright sandstone to the left. It is possible to continue down the valley and join the La Madre Spring Trail. A complete loop can be done by using the White Rock Spring Trail to return to the starting point.

HIKE 69 *WHITE ROCK SPRING*

General description: A day hike in the Red Rock Canyon National Conservation Area.

General location: Approximately 15 miles west of Las Vegas.

Maps: La Madre Mtn 7.5-minute USGS.

Difficulty: Easy.

Length: 0.3 mile one way.

Elevation: 4,800 feet.

Special attractions: Opportunity to observe bighorn sheep.

Water: None.

Best season: Fall through spring.

For more information: Red Rock Canyon National Conservation Area, Bureau of Land Management, P.O. Box 26569, Las Vegas, NV 89126; (702) 363-1921.

Permit: None (day use only).

Finding the trailhead: Follow the description for Hike 63 Moenkopi Trail to reach the BLM visitor center. Then continue on the loop road (one way) to the lower White Rock Springs parking area and turn right. Drive the dirt road 0.8 mile to its end and park.

The hike: The trail is a closed dirt road on the left (west). Follow the old road to the water catchment constructed by the Civilian Conservation Corps. This is a good place to observe bighorn sheep, in season.

Water catchments such as this one are intended to expand the range of the desert bighorn sheep by providing additional permanent water sources. This enables the animals to use more of their natural habitat.—*Bureau of Land Management and Bruce Grubbs*

HIKE 70 *WHITE ROCK SPRING TO WILLOW SPRING*

General description: A day hike in the Red Rock Canyon National Conservation Area.

General location: Approximately 15 miles west of Las Vegas.

Maps: La Madre Mtn 7.5-minute USGS.

Difficulty: Easy.

Length: 1.5 miles one way.

Elevation: 4,800 to 4,400 feet.

Special attractions: Connection between White Rock Spring and Willow Spring trails.

Water: None.

Best season: Fall through spring.

For more information: Red Rock Canyon National Conservation Area, Bureau of Land Management, P.O. Box 26569, Las Vegas, NV 89126; (702) 363-1921.

Permit: None (day use only).

Finding the trailhead: Follow the description for Hike 63 Moenkopi Trail to reach the Bureau of Land Management Visitor Center. Then continue on the loop road (one way) to the lower White Rock Springs parking area and turn right. Drive the dirt road 0.8 mile to its end and park.

The hike: The trail is the closed dirt road on the left (west). Follow the closed dirt road toward the water catchment (see Hike 69 White Rock Spring Trail). Just before reaching the catchment, the trail to Willow Spring can be located on the left, heading in a southwesterly direction. The trail follows along the base of the White Rock Hills and joins the Willow Spring Trail across from the Lost Creek parking area.

Along this trail or almost anywhere in the Nevada desert you are likely see one of the American desert's most common mammals—the jackrabbit with its large, black tipped ears. It is commonly seen bounding across roads, and in good years is unusually numerous.

The large ears contain many blood vessels and serve to radiate heat to the environment to cool the animal.—*Bureau of Land Management and Bruce Grubbs*

The falls in Lost Creek, in the Red Rock Canyon National Conservation Area, are seasonal although a short distance downstream Lost Creek has a permanent flow of water. This waterfall blocks access to the upper part of the canyon.

HIKE 71 *LOST CREEK LOOP*

General description: A day hike in the Red Rock Canyon National Conservation Area.

General location: Approximately 15 miles west of Las Vegas.

Maps: La Madre Mtn. 7.5-minute USGS.

Difficulty: Easy.

Length: 0.7 mile loop.

Elevation: 4,400 feet.

Special attractions: Box canyon with a seasonal waterfall.

Water: Lost Creek.

Best season: Fall through spring.

For more information: Red Rock Canyon National Conservation Area, Bureau of Land Management, P.O. Box 26569, Las Vegas, NV 89126; (702) 363-1921.

Permit: None (day use only).

Finding the trailhead: Follow the description for Hike 63 Moenkopi Trail to reach the Bureau of Land Management Visitor Center. Then continue on the loop road (one way) to the Lost Creek parking area and park.

The hike: Take either the right or left loop to the creek, with its permanent water. One can continue upstream to a box canyon with a seasonal waterfall.

A box canyon is a canyon with no outlet at its upper end. Usually the obstacle is a dry waterfall that runs only occasionally.—*Bureau of Land Management and Bruce Grubbs*

HIKE 72 *WILLOW SPRING LOOP*

General description: A day hike in the Red Rock Canyon National Conservation Area.

General location: Approximately 15 miles west of Las Vegas.

Maps: La Madre Mtn. 7.5-minute USGS.

Difficulty: Easy.

Length: 1.5 mile loop.

Elevation: 4,400 feet.

Special attractions: Variety of plant communities—riparian, pines, oaks, and desert.

Water: Willow Spring.

Best season: Fall through spring.

For more information: Red Rock Canyon National Conservation Area, Bureau of Land Management, P.O. Box 26569, Las Vegas, NV 89126; (702) 363-1921.

Permit: None (day use only).

Finding the trailhead: Follow the description for Hike 63 Moenkopi Trail to reach the Bureau of Land Management Visitor Center. Then continue on the loop road (one way) to the Willow Spring Picnic Area and park.

The hike: The trail follows the left (northeast) side of the canyon past Native American roasting pits to the Lost Creek parking area. The right hand trail then crosses Red Rock Wash, branches to the right, and parallels the Red Rock Escarpment and returns to Willow Spring.

Roasting pits were used by the ancient inhabitants for slow-cooking. Agave plants, other vegetables, and meats were placed in a bed of hot coals mixed with cobbles and covered with plant materials and earth. After enough time had passed, the cooked food, ash, and fire-cracked rock were dug out. The discarded rock and ash forms a doughnut shaped ring often several feet high. Also known as mescal pits, these cooking sites are common in the Southwest.—*Bureau of Land Management and Bruce Grubbs*

HIKES 67, 68, 69, 70, 71, 72, & 76

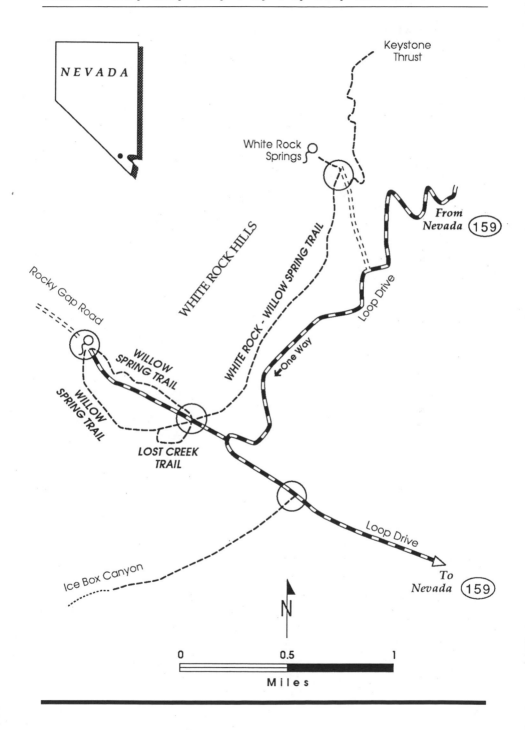

NEVADA

Keystone Thrust

White Rock Springs

WHITE ROCK HILLS

WHITE ROCK - WILLOW SPRING TRAIL

From Nevada (159)

Loop Drive

One Way

Rocky Gap Road

WILLOW SPRING TRAIL

WILLOW SPRING TRAIL

LOST CREEK TRAIL

Loop Drive

To Nevada (159)

Ice Box Canyon

N

0   0.5   1

Miles

HIKE 73 *LA MADRE SPRING*

General description: A day hike in the Red Rock Canyon National Conservation Area.

General location: Approximately 15 miles west of Las Vegas.

Maps: La Madre Mtn. 7.5-minute, La Madre Spring 7.5-minute, Mountain Springs 7.5-minute USGS.

Difficulty: Moderate.

Length: 3 miles one way.

Elevation: 4,400 to 5,360 feet.

Special attractions: Opportunity to view bighorn sheep and other wildlife.

Water: La Madre Spring.

Best season: Fall through spring.

For more information: Red Rock Canyon National Conservation Area, Bureau of Land Management, P.O. Box 26569, Las Vegas, NV 89126; (702) 363-1921.

Permit: None (day use only).

Finding the trailhead: Follow the description for Hike 63 Moenkopi Trail to reach the Bureau of Land Management Visitor Center. Then continue on the loop road (one way) to the Willow Spring Picnic Area and park.

La Madre Spring in the Red Rock Canyon National Conservation Area has been developed as a water source for wildlife.

The hike: Walk up the Rocky Gap Road, an unsigned jeep road that begins at the end of the pavement. Just after crossing the wash turn right at an unsigned fork. A more interesting way to reach this junction is to walk up the wash to the south side of the road. After the fork, stay on the main road, which stays left (west) of the wash. Numerous unsigned roads branch off on either side.

This valley is higher and more sheltered than the open desert east of the White Rock Hills, and so supports a pygmy forest of juniper and singleleaf pinyon pine. The singleleaf pinyon is easily recognized since it is the only pine with needles growing singly rather than in bunches of two or more. Like its cousin the Colorado pinyon, the seeds are edible and used to be an important food source for the native inhabitants. It is still an important food source for birds and small mammals.

The road ends at a small dam, and a foot path leads up the creek to the spring. Bighorn sheep and other wildlife rely on the water from this spring.—*Bureau of Land Management and Bruce Grubbs*

HIKE 74 *TOP OF THE ESCARPMENT*

General description: A day hike in the Red Rock Canyon National Conservation Area.
General location: Approximately 25 miles west of Las Vegas.
Maps: La Madre Mtn. 7.5-minute, La Madre Spring 7.5-minute, Mountain Springs 7.5-minute USGS.
Difficulty: Difficult.
Length: 5 miles one way.
Elevation: 4,400 to 7,500 feet.
Special attractions: Excellent views of the Red Rock Escarpment.
Water: none.
Best season: Summer and fall.
For more information: Red Rock Canyon National Conservation Area, Bureau of Land Management, P.O. Box 26569, Las Vegas, NV 89126; (702) 363-1921.
Permit: Registration required for overnight use.

Finding the trailhead: Follow the description for Hike 63 Moenkopi Trail to reach the Bureau of Land Management Visitor Center. Then continue on the loop road (one way) to the Willow Spring Picnic Area and park. Hike up the Rocky Gap road, a jeep trail which begins at the end of the pavement. Watch for the left (southwest) fork. This four-wheel drive road passes Lone Pine and Switchback Springs as it climbs to Red Rock Summit.

If the road is impassable from Red Rock Summit, about five miles and 3,000 feet elevation gain will be added to the hike to reach Red Rock Summit.

Alternately, Red Rock Summit may be approached from the west. From Las Vegas drive twenty-seven miles west on Nevada Highway 160 to Mountain Springs. Continue about three miles then turn right (north) on the Lovell Canyon road. In approximately eight miles, the road to Red Rock Summit turns right (east). It is about three miles and 1,200 feet of elevation gain to the summit.

The hike: The trail begins at Red Rock Summit and leaves the road to the east. It winds up around the head of a basin that drains to the west and eventually reaches the summit of the escarpment after a mile walk with approximately seven hundred feet of elevation gain.

At the summit, the view encompasses the Spring Mountains to the north, the entire Red Rock Canyon Area, Blue Diamond Mountain, the Las Vegas Valley, Lake Mead, the Mormon Mountains, and Mount Potosi. From the summit follow the ridge east-northeast to another spectacular viewpoint overlooking Red Rock Canyon.—*Bureau of Land Management*

HIKE 75 *BRIDGE MOUNTAIN*

General description: A day hike in the Red Rock Canyon recreation area.
General location: Approximately 25 miles west of Las Vegas.
Maps: Mountain Springs 7.5-minute, La Madre Mtn. 7.5-minute, La Madre Spring 7.5-minute USGS.
Difficulty: Difficult.
Length: 5 miles one way.
Elevation: 4,400 to 7,500 feet (3,800 foot elevation change).
Special attractions: Natural bridge and views of Red Rock Canyon area.
Water: Seasonal in potholes.
Best season: Spring through fall.
For more information: Red Rock Canyon National Conservation Area, Bureau of Land Management, P.O. Box 26569, Las Vegas, NV 89126; (702) 363-1921.
Permit: Registration required for overnight use.

Special instructions: Although this is a day hike of moderate length, the trail is minimal, and the last four hundred-foot climb to the natural bridge on Bridge Mountain is along a steep exposed system of joints and ledges. This section does not require technical climbing equipment or skills, but does require extreme care. Only hikers experienced in cross-country travel should attempt this hike.

Finding the trailhead: Follow the description for Hike 74 Top of the Escarpment.

The hike: The trail begins at Red Rock Summit and leaves the road to the east. It winds up around the head of a basin that drains to the west, and eventually reaches the summit of the escarpment after a mile walk with approximately seven hundred feet of elevation gain.

The trail then turns south along the ridge line for approximately 0.25 mile. It descends around the heads of two small drainages to the east then climbs a steep side hill to the top of a long narrow ridge that runs off to the east into Pine Creek. No trail exists in the resistant sandstone, but the route is intermittently marked by two black parallel lines of paint.

This ridge offers an excellent view of the Keystone Thrust Fault Zone. Tremendous forces associated with the movement of the Earth's crustal plates have forced the dark gray limestones to ride up over the red and white sand-

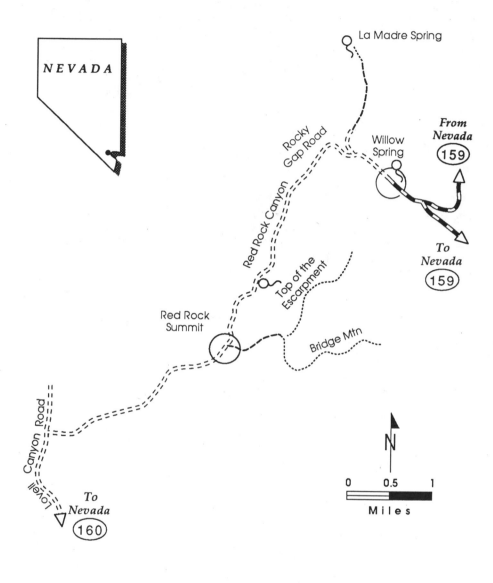

NEVADA

La Madre Spring

Rocky Gap Road

Willow Spring

From Nevada (159)

Red Rock Canyon

To Nevada (159)

Top of the Escarpment

Red Rock Summit

Bridge Mtn

Lovell Canyon Road

To Nevada (160)

N

0   0.5   1

M i l e s

stones that were formed later and were originally positioned above the limestone. The limestone weathers into fairly large blocks that remain in place, trapping sand, silt, and plant debris, which develops into soil that supports a heavy cover of shrubs and small trees. The sandstone weathers differently, breaking down into sand grains that are easily washed and blown away, constantly exposing a new surface of solid rock that is bare of all plants except lichens and a few shrubs growing in cracks. The contrast between the brush covered limestone and the bare sandstone beneath it clearly delineates the Keystone Thrust Fault Zone.

The trail becomes poorly defined as it snakes down the crest of the ridge to the east. Hikers should stay on the crest as much as possible. It is easier along the crest than it is on the side hill. Soon after the limestone disappears and exposes the sandstone, the route drops off the ridge to the north into a small basin that empties into Pine Creek. At the lower edge of the basin, a sheer cliff descends into the depths of Pine Creek 1,500 feet below. Rising air currents are attractive to soaring birds that ride along the cliffs; the rising air also carries flying insects to the higher elevations. Small insect-eating birds such as the white-throated swift and violet green swallow swoop along the edge, buzzing hikers and snapping up bugs on the wing.

From the head of Pine Creek, the route winds off through a slickrock bench studded with numerous small catch basins that hold water after a rain. Some of these basins are quite large; the largest is located in the extreme southeast corner of section 8, near the edge of the Mountain Springs topographic map. Water trapped in these tanks, or tinajas as the Spanish termed them, supports a diverse and fragile community of plants and animals. Ponderosa pines, junipers, pinyon pines, and smaller bushes provide shelter for bird life. Amphibians such as frogs and toads breed in the ponds, and ravens, hawks, deer, bighorn sheep, and hundreds of other animals rely on the tinajas for water. People should never camp within 0.25 mile of such water sources as the presence of humans will scare the wildlife away. Since there is no outlet from the tanks, pollutants from soap, human wastes, or litter will remain in the basins indefinitely, poisoning the creatures that depend on these natural reservoirs.

From the large tank mentioned above, the trail becomes a mere route across the slickrock bench. The correct route is marked intermittently with small patches of orange paint in the shape of bighorn sheep tracks. If the correct route is not followed carefully, hikers will find themselves perched on the edge of a sheer drop with no way down. In many areas, the route is broken by short vertical pitches that must be carefully negotiated. It is approximately 0.5 mile from the big tank to the bottom of the saddle that leads up to Bridge Mountain, with a drop of 350 feet.

To reach the bridge near the summit of Bridge Mountain, the route leads straight up a system of joints and ledges for a distance of four hundred feet. The path is not as sheer as it appears during the approach, and there are plenty of holds for hands and feet. However, the climb is relatively exposed, and extreme care should be exercised during the climb. A misstep could plunge a hiker hundreds of feet into Pine Creek. Climbing within the joints offers more security, but climbing the faces alongside is slightly easier.

Once the bridge has been reached and explored, a further route from inside the alcove near the pine tree leads up onto the bench above. Just one hundred yards north of the bridge is a large, deep, and nearly circular tinaja; it is nearly eighty feet across and sixty feet deep. Over the bench to the east is a large alcove that shelters a hidden forest of ponderosa pines. Trees grow very slowly in this area because of the dry conditions. Wood is relatively scarce, slowly replaced, and absolutely should not be used to build fires. A fire in the hidden forest could cause damage that would not heal in a thousand years. Note that all wood gathering and ground fires are prohibited in the Red Rock backcountry.

Return to Red Rock Summit by retracing your route. Do not attempt to take short cuts or alternate routes.—*Bureau of Land Management*

HIKE 76 *ICE BOX CANYON*

General description: A day hike in the Red Rock Canyon National Conservation Area.

General location: Approximately 20 miles west of Las Vegas.

Maps: La Madre Mtn. 7.5-minute, Mountain Springs 7.5-minute USGS.

Difficulty: Easy.

Length: 1.3 miles one way.

Elevation: 4,300 to 4,600 feet.

Special attractions: Seasonal waterfall and box canyon.

Water: None.

Best season: Spring through fall.

For more information: Red Rock Canyon National Conservation Area, Bureau of Land Management, P.O. Box 26569, Las Vegas, NV 89126; (702) 363-1921.

Permit: None (day use only).

Finding the trailhead: Follow the description for Hike 63 Moenkopi Trail to reach the Bureau of Land Management Visitor Center. Then continue on the loop road (one way) to the Ice Box Canyon Overlook and park.

The hike: Follow the trail across the wash. The trail stays on the bench on the right (north) side of the canyon until the canyon narrows and then ends as it drops into the wash. Follow the wash (boulder hopping is required) to a seasonal waterfall and box canyon. Ice Box Canyon derives its name from the cooler temperatures in this narrow canyon.

These cooler temperatures create what are called micro-climates, small areas where the year-round climate is different enough from the surrounding area to support a plant and animal community normally found at higher elevations.—*Bureau of Land Management and Bruce Grubbs*

An excellent trail leads into Pine Creek Canyon in the Red Rock Canyon National Conservation Area.

HIKE 77 *PINE CREEK CANYON*

General description: A day hike in the Red Rock Canyon National Conservation Area.

General location: Approximately 20 miles west of Las Vegas.

Maps: Blue Diamond 7.5-minute, La Madre Mtn. 7.5-minute, Mountain Springs 7.5-minute USGS.

Difficulty: Easy.

Length: 2.5 miles one way.

Elevation: 4,000 to 5,000 feet.

Special attractions: Unusual low-elevation pine forest.

Water: None.

Best season: Spring through fall.

For more information: Red Rock Canyon National Conservation Area, Bureau of Land Management, P.O. Box 26569, Las Vegas, NV 89126; (702) 363-1921.

Permit: None (day use only).

Finding the trailhead: Follow the description Hike 63 Moenkopi Trail to reach the Bureau of Land Management Visitor Center. Then continue on the loop road (one way) to the Pine Creek Canyon Overlook and park.

The hike: Follow the trail downhill to the closed dirt road that leads to the old Horace Wilson homestead site; nothing remains except the foundation. The canyon divides above the homestead site; either fork can be followed, but the left is preferable. Pine Creek was named for the unusual occurrence of ponderosa pines at this elevation in the desert—the trees thrive here because of the moisture and cooler temperatures.

Here the microclimate supporting the tall pines is caused by the high canyon walls that increase the amount of shade, the moisture from the Pine Creek drainage, and the cool air flowing down the canyon at night. After sunset on calm clear nights, the ground in the high mountains rapidly cools by radiating heat to the open sky. This in turn cools the air in contact with the earth. The cool air is heavier than warmer air and starts to flow downward, collecting in the drainages and moving toward the valleys via the canyons. This is why there is often a down canyon breeze or even a wind in desert canyons and mountain valleys after sunset.—*Bureau of Land Management and Bruce Grubbs*

HIKE 78 *OAK CREEK CANYON*

General description: A day hike in the Red Rock Canyon National Conservation Area.

General location: Approximately 20 miles west of Las Vegas.

Maps: Blue Diamond 7.5-minute USGS.

Difficulty: Easy.

Length: 3 miles one way.

Elevation: 3,760 to 4,800 feet.

Special attractions: Stands of live shrub oak and sandy "beaches" along the wash.

Water: None.

Best season: Spring through fall.

For more information: Red Rock Canyon National Conservation Area, Bureau of Land Management, P.O. Box 26569, Las Vegas, NV 89126; (702) 363-1921.

Permit: None (day use only).

Finding the trailhead: Follow the description for Hike 63 Moenkopi Trail to reach the scenic loop entry, but stay on Nevada Highway 159 south 1.6 miles past the scenic loop exit and turn right (west) onto the dirt road and park.

The hike: Follow the road (very rough four-wheel drive) to the road closure at its end. Now follow the trail around "Potato Knoll" to the left. Oak Creek Canyon is known for its nice stands of live shrub oak and the sandy "beaches" along the wash. Seasonal waterfalls can be found in the canyon.

The term "live oak" means that the plant is evergreen and keeps its leaves all year. Shrub oaks often grow in thick stands with mountain mahogany and manzanita, creating formidable obstacles to cross-country hikers. However, the dense brush provides important cover for wildlife.—*Bureau of Land Management and Bruce Grubbs*

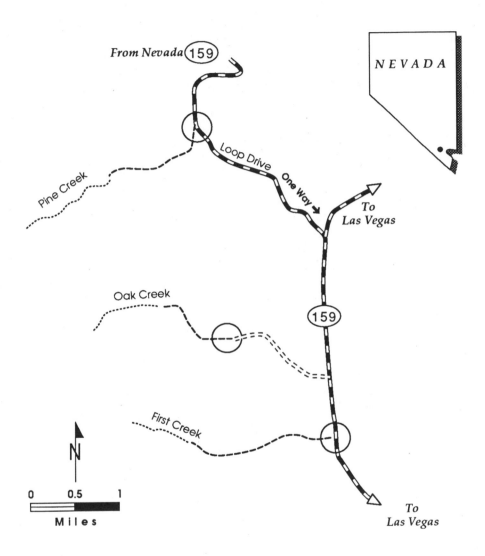

HIKE 79 *FIRST CREEK CANYON*

General description: A day hike in the Red Rock Canyon National Conservation Area.

General location: Approximately 20 miles west of Las Vegas.

Maps: Blue Diamond 7.5-minute, Mountain Springs 7.5-minute USGS.

Difficulty: Moderate.

Length: 2.5 miles one way.

Elevation: 3,650 to 4,800 feet.

Special attractions: Scenic canyon with seasonal waterfalls.

Water: None.

Best season: Spring through fall.

For more information: Red Rock Canyon National Conservation Area, Bureau of Land Management, P.O. Box 26569, Las Vegas, NV 89126; (702) 363-1921.

Permit: None (day use only).

Finding the trailhead: Follow the description for Hike 63 Moenkopi Trail to reach the scenic loop entry but stay on Nevada Highway 159 south 2.6 miles past the scenic loop exit and park in the large dirt parking area.

The hike: Follow the dirt road, which is closed to motorized vehicles, to the mouth of the canyon. A trail follows the left side of the canyon for a distance; some rock scrambling is required thereafter.

Seasonal waterfalls are found all over Nevada in the numberless canyons that cut into the flanks of the mountains. At higher elevations, the falls run during the snowmelt from late spring to early summer and sometimes briefly after heavy thunderstorms. At lower elevations such as these, runoff tends to occur during wet storms, which primarily occur in winter. The best chance to see the falls running is in late winter or early spring.—*Bureau of Land Management and Bruce Grubbs*

HIKE 80 *SPIRIT PEAK*

General description: A cross-country day hike to the highest peak in the Newberry Mountains.

General location: Approximately 10 miles northwest of Laughlin.

Maps: Spirit Mountain 7.5-minute USGS.

Difficulty: Moderate.

Length: 2 miles one way.

Elevation: 3,500 to 5,639 feet.

Special attractions: Rugged granite crags, expansive views of the southern tip of the state.

Water: None.

Best season: Fall through spring.

For more information: Lake Mead National Recreation Area, 601 Nevada Highway, Boulder City, NV 89005; (702) 293-8907.

Permit: None.

Finding the trailhead: From Laughlin, drive west on Nevada Highway 163 approximately six miles to the signed turnoff for Christmas Tree Pass. Turn right on this graded dirt road and continue for 6.2 miles then turn right and continue 0.2 mile to the end of the road.

The view northeast from Spirit Peak in the Newberry Mountains. Lake Mohave on the Colorado River is visible, along with parts of Arizona.

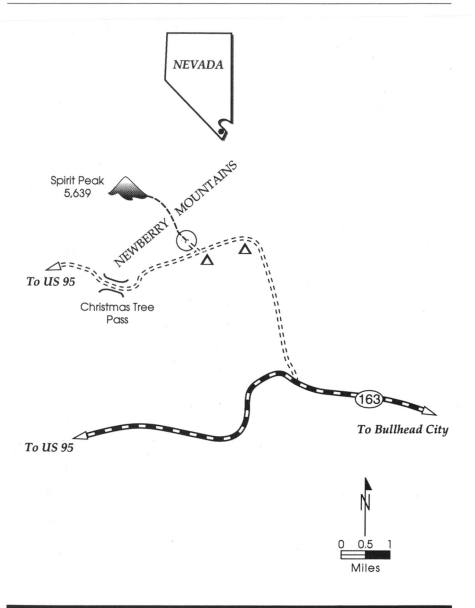

This same turnoff may be reached from the west by leaving U.S. Highway 95 about one mile south of Cal-Nev-Ari and turning east onto the signed Christmas Tree Pass Road, which is maintained gravel. It is approximately ten miles to the trailhead turn off, which is just past the first units of the Christmas Tree Pass Campground.

The hike: Although the summit can be reached many different ways, this is the most direct route. From the parking area, go generally north, angling up the slope toward the last of the granite outcrops on the skyline above. Stay below the steepest terrain near the top of the ridge until nearly to the northern-most visible outcrop then climb an easy gully just to the south of this last outcrop. The top of the ridge is broad and gentle with pleasant little basins.

Notice the gradual change from mesquite desert to pinyon-juniper woodland as you ascend. After wet winters, the ground will be covered with cheat grass, an exotic plant which cures rapidly when the temperature starts to rise in the summer. Once it is completely dry it is a pale yellow or straw color and is extremely flammable. On any slope or with the slightest breeze a wild fire will spread rapidly, burning not only the cheat grass but also the shrubs and trees as well. Most of the native plants are very slow growing and take many years to replace once burned. In dry years, however, there may be almost no cheat grass, leaving the desert nearly fireproof, its more natural state.

Continue directly up the ridge above, going generally west and avoiding rock outcrops to either side. As this ridge joins the main north-south summit ridge angle northwest to reach another pleasant ridgetop. From here, it appears that the summit is the peak to the northeast, but it is actually to the northwest at the end of the very rugged granite ridge. The easiest way to the highest point is to stay below the summits to the north and head diagonally north-west. Skirt the massive granite fins at their southern ends then walk up a gully to a saddle just below the summit. The highest point is marked by an old survey post.

The mountains of four states are spread before you. To the south are the low ranges near Needles, California. The 8,000-foot Hualapai Mountains are visible southeast near Kingman, Arizona. To the northeast, the 8,000-foot Virgin Mountains mark the extreme northwest corner of Arizona. Just beyond the Virgins, the Pine Valley Mountains rise to 10,000 feet above St. George, Utah. Finally, to the northwest, the 11,000-foot Spring Range towers above Las Vegas.

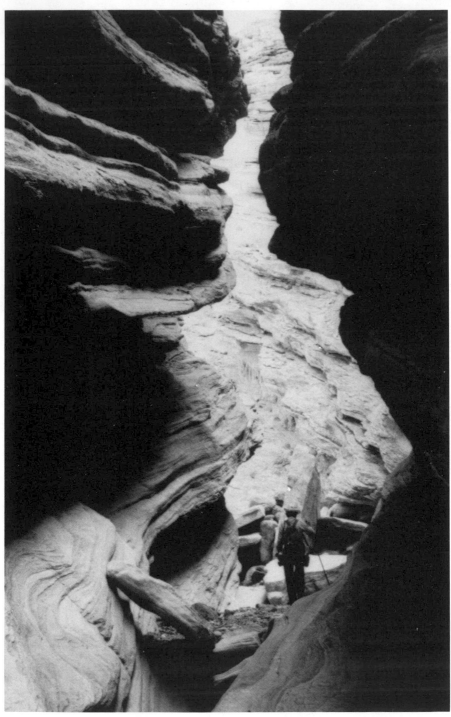

Nevada has over five million acres of land classified as Wilderness Study Areas. Stewart Aitchison photo.

AFTERWORD

Nevada's Wilderness Challenge

Nevada is the most mountainous state, the driest state, and the fastest growing state in the country. Until recently, its vast wild places were relatively unknown except to a few hardy souls (including John Muir). Now, growing numbers of hikers are discovering the beautiful expanses of high desert and unique mountain ranges of Nevada.

On December 5, 1989, President Bush signed the Nevada Wilderness Bill, incorporating 732,000 acres of USDA Forest Service land into the National Wilderness System. The bill was the result of a twenty-five-year campaign to achieve formal wilderness designation for some magnificent wildlands. Prior to this date the 64,000 acre Jarbidge Wilderness, grandfathered in under the 1964 Wilderness Act, represented the sum total of Nevada wilderness. Conservationists pushed for a 1.4 million acre bill and will work in the future to include most of the 700,000 acres omitted in the legislation.

But a far bigger battle is in store. Except for Alaska, Nevada has the largest amount of area managed by the Bureau of Land Management and has more than five million acres of lands classified as Wilderness Study Areas. Approximately two million acres are recommended by the BLM itself. These areas range from the spectacular forested peak of 10,990-foot Mount Grafton in eastern Nevada to the enormous expanse of the Black Rock Desert in north-

Many of Nevada's mountains are now protected in the National Wilderness Preservation System. In Wilderness, only foot and horse travel are allowed. All forms of mechanized travel, including bicycles, are prohibited. This not only ensures a primitive backcountry setting for those who desire it, but also protects vital wildlife habitat.

western Nevada and to the red rock country of the Muddy and Mormon mountains in southern Nevada. It will take a strong and united effort on the part of conservationists and hikers to achieve wilderness status for these remote lands. In addition, both the Sheldon National Wildlife Refuge and the Desert National Wildlife Refuge have hundreds of thousands of acres of de facto wilderness.

The potential for a real wilderness base in Nevada is unlimited. However, it will take hard work and probably many years to achieve. In the meantime, we need wilderness enthusiasts to get out and enjoy what Nevada has to offer and spread the word to others.—*Marjorie Sill*

HIKER'S CHECKLIST

This checklist may be useful for ensuring that nothing essential is forgotten. Of course, it contains far more items than are needed on any individual hiking trip.

Clothing

- ☐ Shirt
- ☐ Pants
- ☐ Underwear (extra)
- ☐ Swim suit
- ☐ Walking shorts
- ☐ Belt or suspenders
- ☐ Windbreaker Jacket or parka
- ☐ Rain gear
- ☐ Gloves or mittens
- ☐ Sun hat
- ☐ Warm cap for cold
- ☐ Bandanna
- ☐ Sweater

Footwear

- ☐ Boots
- ☐ Socks (extra)
- ☐ Boot wax
- ☐ Camp shoes

Sleeping

- ☐ Tarp or tent with fly
- ☐ Groundsheet
- ☐ Sleeping pad
- ☐ Sleeping bag

Packing

- ☐ Backpack
- ☐ Day pack or fanny pack

Cooking

- ☐ Matches or lighter
- ☐ Waterproof match case
- ☐ Fire starter
- ☐ Stove
- ☐ Fuel
- ☐ Stove maintenance kit
- ☐ Cooking pot(s)
- ☐ Cup
- ☐ Bowl or plate
- ☐ Utensils
- ☐ Pot scrubber
- ☐ Plastic water bottles
- ☐ Collapsible water containers

Food

- ☐ Cereal
- ☐ Bread
- ☐ Crackers
- ☐ Cheese
- ☐ Margarine
- ☐ Dry soup
- ☐ Packaged dinners
- ☐ Snacks
- ☐ Hot chocolate
- ☐ Tea
- ☐ Powdered milk
- ☐ Powdered drink mixes

Navigation
- [ ] Topographic maps
- [ ] Compass

Emergency/Repair
- [ ] Pocket knife
- [ ] First aid kit
- [ ] Snakebite kit
- [ ] Nylon cord
- [ ] Plastic bags
- [ ] Wallet or ID card
- [ ] Coins for phone calls
- [ ] Space blanket
- [ ] Emergency fishing gear
- [ ] Signal mirror
- [ ] Pack parts
- [ ] Stove parts
- [ ] Tent parts
- [ ] Flashlight bulbs, batteries
- [ ] Scissors
- [ ] Safety pins

Car
- [ ] Extra water
- [ ] Extra food
- [ ] Extra clothes

Miscellaneous
- [ ] Fishing gear
- [ ] Photographic gear
- [ ] Sunglasses
- [ ] Flashlight
- [ ] Candle lantern
- [ ] Sunscreen
- [ ] Insect repellent
- [ ] Toilet paper an
- [ ] Binoculars
- [ ] Trash bags
- [ ] Notebook and pencils
- [ ] Field guides
- [ ] Book or game
- [ ] Dental and personal items
- [ ] Trowel
- [ ] Towel
- [ ] Water purification tablets
- [ ] Car key
- [ ] Watch
- [ ] Calendar

RESOURCES

Conservation Organizations and Hiking Clubs

Desert Trail Association, P.O. Box 537, Burns, OR 97720

Friends of Nevada Wilderness, P.O. Box 19777, Las Vegas, NV 89132

Nevada Outdoor Recreation, Association, Box 1245, Carson City, NV 89702

Nevada Trails Coalition, HCR 38 Box 325, Las Vegas, NV 89124; (702) 252-5082.

Sierra Club, 5428 College Ave, Oakland, CA 94618; (415) 654-7847

Sierra Club, 730 Polk St., San Francisco, CA 94109; (415) 981-8634

Sierra Club, Angeles Chapter, 2410 W. Beverly Blvd., Suite 2, Los Angeles, CA 90057; (213) 387-4287

Sierra Club, Mother Lode Chapter, P.O. Box 1335, Sacramento, CA 95806; (916) 444-2180

Sierra Club, Toiyabe Chapter, Box 8096, Reno, NV 89507

Tahoe Rim Trail, P.O. Box 10156, S. Lake Tahoe, CA 95731; (916) 577-8783

Nevada Division of State Parks

Nevada Division of State Parks, 1060 Mallory Way, Carson City, NV 89701; (702) 885-4379

Nevada Division of State Parks, 123 W. Nye Lane, Carson City, NV 89710; (702) 687-4370

Nevada Division of State Parks, 4747 Vegas Dr., Las Vegas, NV 89108; (702) 486-5126

Tribal Governments

Pyramid Lake Paiute Tribe, P.O. Box 256, Nixon, NV 89424; (702) 574-0140

Bureau of Land Management

Battle Mountain District Office, 2nd and Scott Street, P.O. Box 1420, Battle Mountain, NV 89820; (702) 631-5181

Carson City District Office, 1535 Hot Springs Rd., #300, Carson City, NV 89701; (702) 882-1631

Elko District Office, 3900 E. Idaho St., P.O. Box 831, Elko, NV 89801; (702) 738-4071

Ely District Office, Pioche Hwy., Star Route 5, Box 1, Ely, NV 89301; (702) 289-4865

Las Vegas District Office, 4765 Vegas Dr., P.O. Box 5408, Las Vegas, NV 89108; (702) 646-8800

Nevada State Office, 850 Harvard Way, P.O. Box 12000, Reno, NV 89520; (702) 784-5748

Red Rock Canyon National Conservation Area, P.O. Box 26569, Las Vegas, NV 89126; (702) 363-1921

Susanville District Office, P.O. Box 1090, 705 Hall St., Susanville, CA 96130; (916) 257-5385

Winnemucca District Office, 705 E. 4th St., Winnemucca, NV 89445; (702) 623-1500

U.S. Fish and Wildlife Service

Ruby Lake National Wildlife Refuge, Ruby Valley, NV 89833; (702) 779-2237

Desert National Wildlife Refuge, 1500 N. Decatur Blvd., Las Vegas, NV 89108; (702) 646-3401

Sheldon National Wildlife Refuge, P.O. Box 111, Lakeview, OR 97630; (503) 947-3315

U.S. Fish and Wildlife Service, 4600 Kietzke Ln., Bldg C Room 120, Reno, NV 89502; (702) 784-5227

USDA Forest Service

Humboldt National Forest, Ely Ranger District, 350 E. 8th, P.O. Box 539, Ely, NV 89301; (702) 289-3031

Humboldt National Forest, Jarbidge Ranger District, 1008 Burley Ave, Buhl, ID 83316-1812; (208) 543-4129

Humboldt National Forest, Mountain City Ranger District, P.O. Box 276, Mountain City, NV 89831; (702) 763-6691

Humboldt National Forest, Santa Rosa Ranger District, 1200 E. Winnemucca Blvd., Winnemucca, NV 89445; (702) 623-5025

Humboldt National Forest, Supervisors Office, 976 Mountain City Hwy., Elko, NV 89801; (702) 738-5171

Humboldt National Forest, Wells Ranger District, Wells, NV 89825; (702) 752-3357

Intermountain Regional Office, 324 - 25th St., Ogden, UT 84401; (801) 625-5182

Toiyabe National Forest, Austin Ranger District, Austin, NV 89310; (702) 964-2671

Toiyabe National Forest, Bridgeport Ranger District, P.O. Box 595, Bridgeport, CA 93517; (714) 932-7070

Toiyabe National Forest, Carson Ranger District, 1536 S. Carson St., Carson City, NV 89701; (702) 882-2766

Toiyabe National Forest, Las Vegas Ranger District, 2881 S. Valley View, Suite 16, Las Vegas, NV 89104; (702) 873-8800

Toiyabe National Forest, Supervisor's Office, 1200 Franklin Way, Sparks, NV 89431; (702) 784-5331

Toiyabe National Forest, Tonopah Ranger District, P.O. Box 3940, Tonopah, NV 89049-3940; (702) 482-6286

National Park Service

Great Basin National Park, Baker, NV 89311; (702) 234-7331

Lake Mead National Recreation Area, 601 Nevada Highway, Boulder City, NV 89005; (702) 293-8907

FURTHER READING

Cline, Gloria Griffen. *Exploring the Great Basin*. University of Nevada Press: Reno, Nevada, 1963.

Elliott, Russel R. *History of Nevada*. University of Nebraska Press: Lincoln, Nebraska, 1987.

Fiero, G. William. *Nevada's Valley of Fire*. KC Publications, Las Vegas, Nevada, 1991.

Hart, John. *Hiking the Great Basin*. Sierra Club, San Francisco, California, 1981.

Houghton, Samuel G. *A Trace of Desert Waters: The Great Basin Story*. Howe Brothers, Salt Lake City, Utah, 1986.

Larson, Peggy. *The Sierra Club Naturalist's Guide to the Deserts of the Southwest*. Sierra Club Books, San Francisco, California, 1977.

Perry, John and Jane Greverus. *Guide to the Natural Areas of New Mexico, Arizona, and Nevada*. Sierra Club Books, San Francisco, California, 1985.

Redfern, Ron. *The Making of a Continent*. Times Books: New York, Redfern, Ron. The Making of a Continent. Times Books: New York, New York, 1983.

Wilkerson, James. *Medicine for Mountaineering*. The Mountaineers: Seattle, Washington, 1985.

FINDING MAPS

USDA Forest Service maps for the state of Nevada may be obtained from the Intermountain Regional Office (see RESOURCES) , as well as from most ranger stations. Also, local hiking shops often stock Forest Service maps.

Bureau of Land Management maps may be obtained from the District offices listed under Resources, and from the U.S. Geological Survey (see below).

Topographic maps may be obtained from the U.S. Geological Survey, Distribution Branch, Box 25286, Denver Federal Center, Denver, CO 80225. Request the free Nevada indexes and order forms for 7.5 and 15-minute topographic maps, as well as 1:125,000 topographic and planimetric maps. The 1:125,000 index also covers Bureau of Land Management maps. Many hiking shops and some engineering supply shops also stock 7.5 and 15-minute topographic maps. Note that while some of the hikes refer to 15-minute maps, these older maps are being rapidly replaced by the newer and more detailed 7.5-minute maps. Before ordering or buying a 15-minute map, check to see if a 7.5-minute is available.

ABOUT THE AUTHOR

Bruce Grubbs has been actively backpacking and hiking in the Southwest for more than twenty-five years. He has written one previous book, *The Hiker's Guide to Arizona*, with Stewart Aitchison. He lives in Flagstaff, Arizona, and is a commercial pilot for a commuter airline.

MAP INDEX

DENNIS COELLO'S AMERICA BY MOUNTAIN BIKE SERIES

Happy Trails

Hop on your mountain bike and let our guidebooks take you on America's classic trails and rides. These "where-to" books are published jointly by Falcon Press and Menasha Ridge Press and written by local biking experts. Twenty regional books will blanket the country when the series is complete.

Choose from an assortment of rides—easy rambles to all-day treks. Guides contain helpful trail and route descriptions, mountain bike shop listings, and interesting facts on area history. Each trail is described in terms of difficulty, scenery, condition, length, and elevation change. The guides also explain trail hazards, nearby services and ranger stations, how much water to bring, and what kind of gear to pack.

So before you hit the trail, grab one of our guidebooks to help make your outdoor adventures safe and memorable.

Call or write
Falcon Press or Menasha Ridge Press
Falcon Press
P.O. Box 1718, Helena, MT 59624
1-800-582-2665
Menasha Ridge Press
3169 Cahaba Heights Road, Birmingham, AL 35243
1-800-247-9437

FALCON PRESS

Menasha Ridge Press

FALCONGUIDES *Perfect for every outdoor adventure!*

FISHING
Angler's Guide to Alaska
Angler's Guide to Montana

FLOATING
Floater's Guide to Colorado
Floater's Guide to Missouri
Floater's Guide to Montana

HIKING
Hiker's Guide to Alaska
Hiker's Guide to Alberta
Hiker's Guide to Arizona
Hiker's Guide to California
Hiker's Guide to Colorado
Hiker's Guide to Florida
Hiker's Guide to Georgia
Hiker's Guide to Hot Springs
  in the Pacific Northwest
Hiker's Guide to Idaho
Hiker's Guide to Montana
Hiker's Guide to Montana's
  Continental Divide Trail
Hiker's Guide to Nevada
Hiker's Guide to New Mexico
Hiker's Guide to North Carolina
Hiker's Guide to Oregon
Hiker's Guide to Texas
Hiker's Guide to Utah
Hiker's Guide to Virginia
Hiker's Guide to Washington
Hiker's Guide to Wyoming
Trail Guide to Glacier/Waterton
  National Parks
Wild Country Companion

MOUNTAIN BIKING
Mountain Biker's Guide to Arizona
Mountain Biker's Guide to
  Central Appalachia
Mountain Biker's Guide to Colorado
Mountain Biker's Guide to New Mexico
Mountain Biker's Guide to Northern
  California/Nevada
Mountain Biker's Guide to Northern
  New England
Mountain Biker's Guide to the
  Northern Rockies
Mountain Biker's Guide to the Ozarks

Mountain Biker's Guide to
  the Southeast
Mountain Biker's Guide to
  Southern California
Mountain Biker's Guide to Southern
  New England

ROCKHOUNDING
Rockhound's Guide to Arizona
Rockhound's Guide to Montana

SCENIC DRIVING
Arizona Scenic Drives
Back Country Byways
California Scenic Drives
Colorado Scenic Drives
New Mexico Scenic Drives
Oregon Scenic Drives
Scenic Byways
Scenic Byways II
Trail of the Great Bear
Traveler's Guide to the Oregon Trail
Traveler's Guide to the
  Lewis and Clark Trail

WILDLIFE VIEWING GUIDES
Arizona Wildlife Viewing Guide
California Wildlife Viewing Guide
Colorado Wildlife Viewing Guide
Florida Wildlife Viewing Guide
Idaho Wildlife Viewing Guide
Indiana Wildlife Viewing Guide
Montana Wildlife Viewing Guide
Nevada Wildlife Viewing Guide
New Mexico Wildlife Viewing Guide
North Carolina Wildlife Viewing Guide
North Dakota Wildlife Viewing Guide
Oregon Wildlife Viewing Guide
Tennessee Wildlife Viewing Guide
Texas Wildlife Viewing Guide
Utah Wildlife Viewing Guide
Washington Wildlife Viewing Guide

PLUS—
Birder's Guide to Montana
Hunter's Guide to Montana
Recreation Guide to
  California National Forests
Recreation Guide to Washington
  National Forests